THE BIG BOOK OF BIBLE CRAFTS AND PROJECTS

WRITTEN BY
JOY MACKENZIE

ILLUSTRATED BY
RUSS FLINT

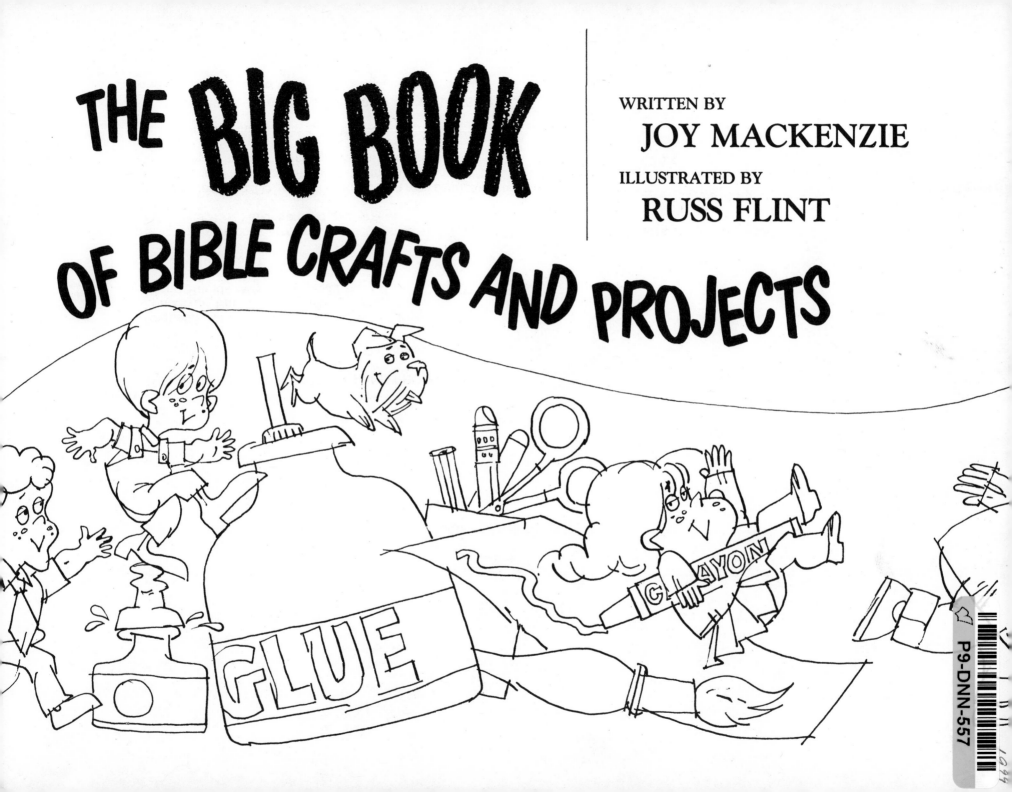

THE BIG BOOK OF BIBLE CRAFTS AND PROJECTS

Copyright © 1982 by The Zondervan Corporation

Requests for information should be addressed to:
Zondervan Publishing House
Grand Rapids, Michigan 49530

ISBN 0-310-70151-1

Scripture references marked LB are taken from *The Living Bible,* paraphrased (Wheaton: Tyndale House
Publishers, 1971) and are used by permission.

Printed in the United States of America

96 97 98 99 00 01 02 / ❖ ML / 18 17 16 15 14 13 12

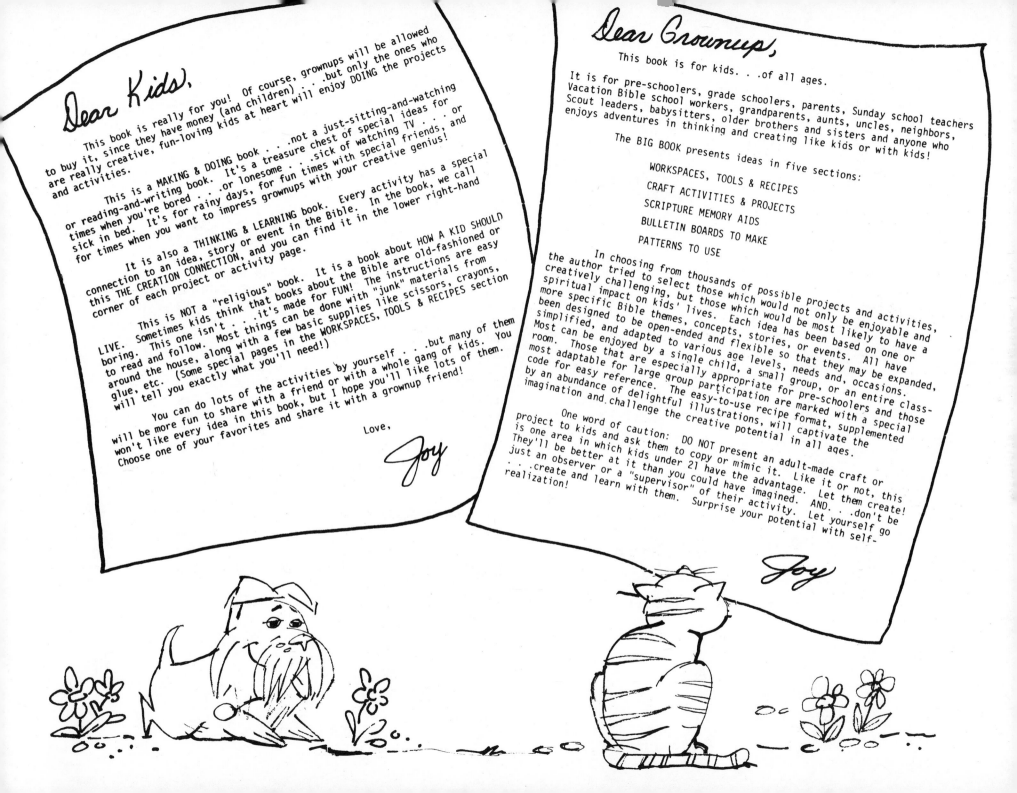

Dear Kids,

This book is really for you! Of course, grownups will be allowed to buy it, since they have money (and children) . . .but only the ones who are really creative, fun-loving kids at heart will enjoy DOING the projects and activities.

This is a MAKING & DOING book . . .not a just-sitting-and-watching or reading-and-writing book. It's a treasure chest of special ideas for times when you're bored . . .or lonesome . . .sick of watching TV . . . or sick in bed. It's for rainy days, for fun times with special friends, and for times when you want to impress grownups with your creative genius!

It is also a THINKING & LEARNING book. Every activity has a special connection to an idea, story or event in the Bible. In the book, we call this THE CREATION CONNECTION, and you can find it in the lower right-hand corner of each project or activity page.

This is NOT a "religious" book. It is a book about HOW A KID SHOULD LIVE. Sometimes kids think that books about the Bible are old-fashioned or boring. This one isn't . . .it's made for FUN! The instructions are easy to read and follow. Most things can be done with "junk" materials from around the house, along with a few basic supplies like scissors, crayons, glue, etc. (Some special pages in the WORKSPACES, TOOLS & RECIPES section will tell you exactly what you'll need!)

You can do lots of the activities by yourself . . .but many of them will be more fun to share with a friend or with a whole gang of kids. You won't like every idea in this book, but I hope you'll like lots of them. Choose one of your favorites and share it with a grownup friend!

Love,

Joy

Dear Grownups,

This book is for kids. . .of all ages.

It is for pre-schoolers, grade schoolers, parents, Sunday school teachers Vacation Bible school workers, grandparents, aunts, uncles, neighbors, Scout leaders, babysitters, older brothers and sisters and anyone who enjoys adventures in thinking and creating like kids or with kids!

The BIG BOOK presents ideas in five sections:

WORKSPACES, TOOLS & RECIPES

CRAFT ACTIVITIES & PROJECTS

SCRIPTURE MEMORY AIDS

BULLETIN BOARDS TO MAKE

PATTERNS TO USE

In choosing from thousands of possible projects and activities, the author tried to select those which would not only be enjoyable and creatively challenging, but those which would be most likely to have a spiritual impact on kids' lives. Each idea has been based on one or more specific Bible themes, concepts, stories, or events. All have been designed to be open-ended and flexible so that they may be expanded, simplified, and adapted to various age levels, needs and, occasions. Most can be enjoyed by a single child, a small group, or an entire class-room. Those that are especially appropriate for pre-schoolers and those most adaptable for large group participation are marked with a special code for easy reference. The easy-to-use recipe format, supplemented by an abundance of delightful illustrations, will captivate the imagination and challenge the creative potential in all ages.

One word of caution: DO NOT present an adult-made craft or project to kids and ask them to copy or mimic it. Like it or not, this is one area in which kids under 21 have the advantage. Let them create! They'll be better at it than you could have imagined. AND. . .don't be just an observer or a "supervisor" of their activity. Let yourself go . . .create and learn with them. Surprise your potential with self-realization!

Joy

TABLE OF CONTENTS

TABLE OF CONTENTS

TABLE OF CONTENTS

EXPLANATION OF CODE: Pages displaying the following symbols indicate activities especially suitable for GROUPS or YOUNG CHILDREN (ages 3-6).

 YOUNG CHILDREN    GROUP ACTIVITY

QUIET PLACES FOR...

If you don't have a special private workspace where you can think great thoughts and create wonderful product, try one of these!

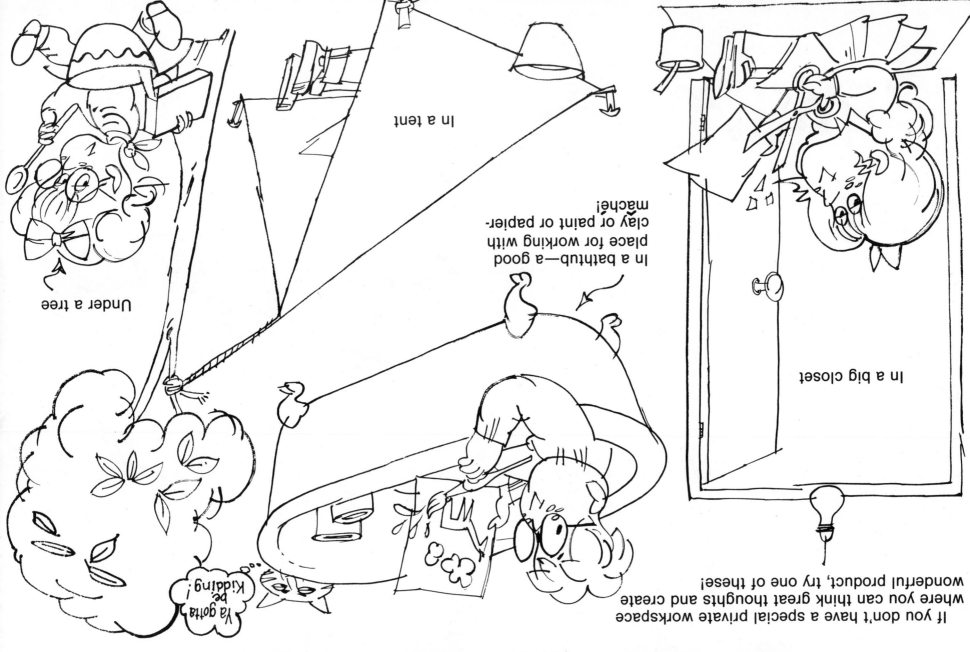

Under a tree

In a tent

In a bathtub—a good place for working with clay or paint or papier-mâché!

In a big closet

Ya gotta be Kidding!

8

WORKSPACES

In a big box

Behind a screen

Under a desk or table

Behind a couch or chair

9

CONSTRUCTION KIT

CONSTRUCTION KIT

You can make up your very own construction kit by buying an inexpensive, plastic cleaning caddy (with a center handle) or by recycling a cardboard soft-drink carton.

Decorate your kit to make it "arty" and interesting. Then fill it with all sorts of magic stuff like crayons, scissors, pencils, felt-tip pens, stickers, tape, bits of cloth, paste, string, cotton balls, brass fasteners, 3x5 cards, a stapler, nails, a dull knife, yarn, cotton balls, etc.

Check the supply list on the next page to see what other things you need to collect for the projects in this book.

HEY WART! COME BACK HERE WITH THAT TOOL KIT... EVERYTHING I NEED IS IN THERE!

PASTE

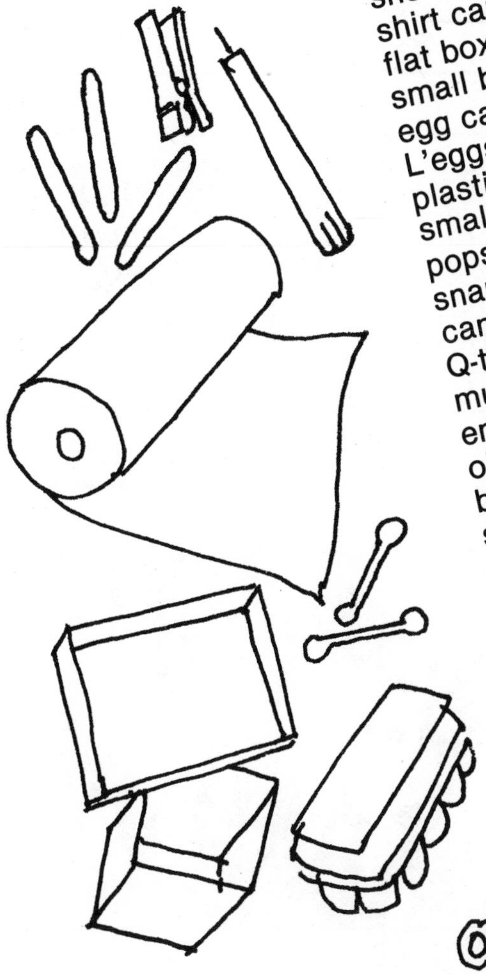

colored construction paper
brown wrapping paper
shelf paper
shirt cardboards
flat boxes
small boxes
egg cartons
L'eggs stocking eggs
plastic detergent bottles
small plastic containers with lids
popsicle sticks
snap-on clothespins
cans with plastic lids
Q-tips
muffin tins
empty roll-on deodorant bottles
old candles
buttons
safety pins
macaroni
ribbon and laces
toothpicks
straws
crepe paper
bricks
seeds
rubber and elastic bands

fabric scraps
sponges
spools
paper cups and plates
styrofoam meat trays
cardboard tubes
hangers
old gloves
old socks, stockings
toothpaste
newspapers
magazines
tissue paper
scrap lumber
sand paper
colored chalk
chicken wire
cassette tapes
plastic sandwich bags
paper bags
modeling clay
art gum
glitter

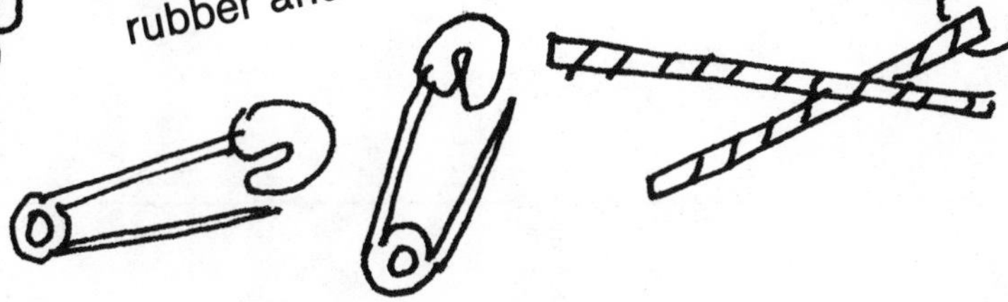

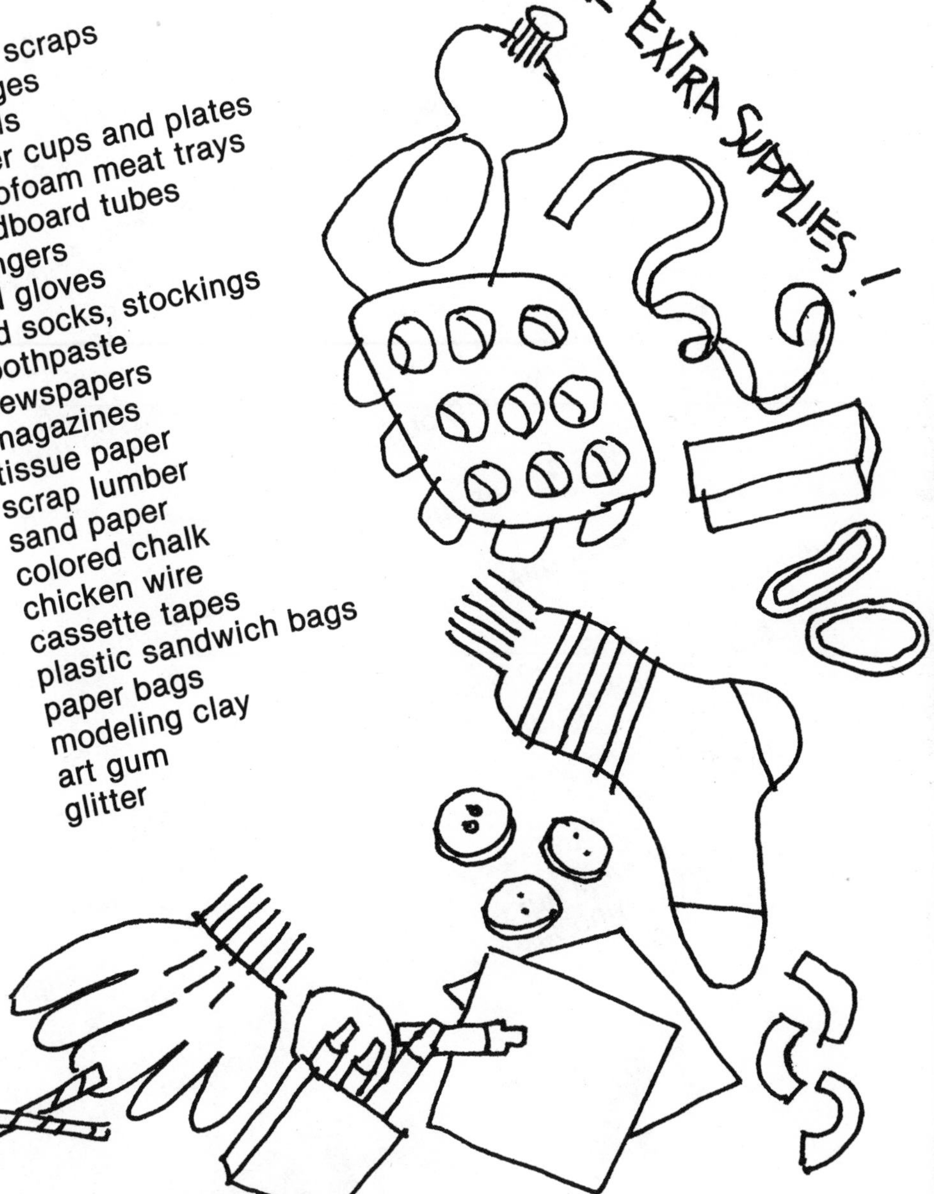

ACTIVITY TIMES WILL BE CLEANER AND HAPPIER IF YOU...

- work on vinyl tablecloths OR an old shower curtain OR slit two sides of giant leaf and trash bags to spread in the work area
- paint with sponges, Q-tips, or a separate brush for each color
- spread glue with Q-tips, small sponge pieces, or paint brushes
- use muffin cups or plastic egg cartons for separate paint colors
- store paint in old mustard or ketchup squeeze bottles OR liquid soap bottles OR roll-on deodorant bottles
- use Dad's old T-shirts OR plastic garbage bags with holes cut for head and arms as aprons
- add a few drops of liquid soap to tempera paints to help it cover bottles and cans
- keep lids of paint jars from sticking by greasing them with Vaseline
- spray chalk drawings with evaporated milk for long life
- add a few drops of bath oil, perfume, or oil of peppermint to play clay to keep it from molding
- don't pour plaster down a sink drain. It will harden and create a horrible, no good, very bad problem!
- dry paintings on a clothesline or collapsible drying rack OR flat on the floor
- put away tools and materials and clean up workspaces (including the floor) when you are finished. Don't forget to clean up your own face and hands too!
- always ask for help when using things that could be dangerous—like candles, knives, ovens, irons, plastic bags, sharp cutting tools

IS THAT TO KEEP YOU CLEAN?

I CUT ARM HOLES - & A HEAD HOLE IN A PLASTIC BAG. I CRACKLE BUT I'M CLEAN!

YOU WILL NEED

Self-adhesive plastic
    coverings in various
    colors and patterns
Colorful, "fun" pictures
Clear adhesive covering
Scissors

THEN . . .

Make a plain, dull work
space bright and cheer-
ful!

Cover a special work
area with plastic strips
and pieces, cut and laid
in patchwork fashion.

Add pictures and cover
over with clear adhesive
covering.

BRIGHTEN THE CORNER WHERE YOU WORK

I ALREADY HAVE... SHE EVEN GAVE US PERMISSION TO DECORATE IT!

FIRST, LET'S ASK MOM IF WE CAN USE THIS OLD TABLE.

N CONNECTION

the CREATIO

WATCH FOR IT!

COMING SOON TO THIS LOCATION "CREATION CONNECTION"

13

while You Work...

WHILE YOU WORK . . .

Doing the crafts and projects in this book just might be so much fun that you could easily forget to do some of the usually important things in your life . . . like eating, for instance.

Just in case that should happen, make this emergency provision:

Use a *sandwich bag* to collect "yummies for the tummy" such as *Cheerios* and other *cereals, miniature marshmallows, cheese puffs, raisins, dried fruit, popcorn,* etc.

String the goodies on a heavy *thread* or piece of *dental floss* with a *darning needle.*

Tie it around your neck and nibble while you work!!

Note: *A whole group of kids might make goody necklaces and nibble while they listen to a story.*

It is also a great idea for snack breaks in Sunday school or vacation Bible school.

...a goody necklace

RECIPES

PLAY CLAY
2 cups flour
1 cup salt
1 cup water
food coloring
bath oil, peppermint oil, or perfume

Mix flour and salt. Add water slowly and squish the mixture between your fingers until it makes dough. Knead in 2 or 3 drops of food coloring and a splotch of bath or peppermint oil to make it smell good. Store in airtight container such as plastic margarine tub or Zip-loc freezer bags.

PRIMARY PASTE
Mix ½ cup water and 1 cup flour together in a bowl. Spoon into a jar or sqeeze bottle to store.

PASTE FOR PAPIER MÂCHÉ
3 cups water
1½ cups flour
oil of peppermint

Mix flour with cold water. Cook over low heat, stirring until paste thickens. (If it gets too thick, add a little water.) Cool the mixture and add 1 teaspoon of peppermint oil.

FINGER PAINT — 4 WAYS
Use pudding! (You can lick the "paint" off your fingers!)

OR

Mix liquid starch and food coloring

OR

Mix wheat paste and water with tempera paint

OR

Mix 3 T sugar with ½ cup cornstarch and 2 cups of cold water. Cook over low heat, stirring until thick. Cool and pour into muffin tins. Add powdered tempera or food coloring to each muffin cup to create separate colors.

VARIATIONS ON PAINT
Make some magic by adding these things to powdered tempera paint:

1. a large dose of liquid detergent. Use in heavy globs to create an oil painting effect.
2. any detergent to prevent cracking and make it easier to wash out.
3. liquid starch to make it thicker.
4. alum to preserve it.
5. condensed milk to make it glossier.
6. salt, sawdust, coffee grounds to create texture.
7. dry corn meal. Sprinkle over areas painted with thinned white glue for a "sand" look. (Shake off excess.)
8. salt. Pour dry mixture into a shaker. Shake over wet paper to create an interesting color effect.
9. soapflakes or liquid detergent and beat until fluffy to make thick, foamy paint.
10. 3 parts water to 1 part tempera to make a *thin wash.*

Frames & Borders

You can make your paintings and drawings very special by mounting them and giving them unusual mats, frames, or borders. Several ways of making borders are illustrated on this page. Try several of them with your favorite masterpieces!

Lay a stiff, neatly cut piece of cardboard or heavy paper exactly in the middle of a piece of poster board the same size as your painting. Roll or sponge paint around the edges like this. Then remove the cardboard and cut out the blank space. Shazam! A border!

Stencil a border by cutting shapes in a lightweight cardboard. Lay it securely on the "frame" and paint over it. Remove the stencil carefully to see your design.

Cut a poster board frame for your picture. Glue patterns of string or yarn, buttons, beads, or a mosaic design of macaroni to your frame.

YOUR PAINTING

CARDBOARD OR HEAVY PAPER

WEIGHT

POSTER BOARD SAME SIZE AS PAINTING

NOW DAB SPONGE WITH PAINT!

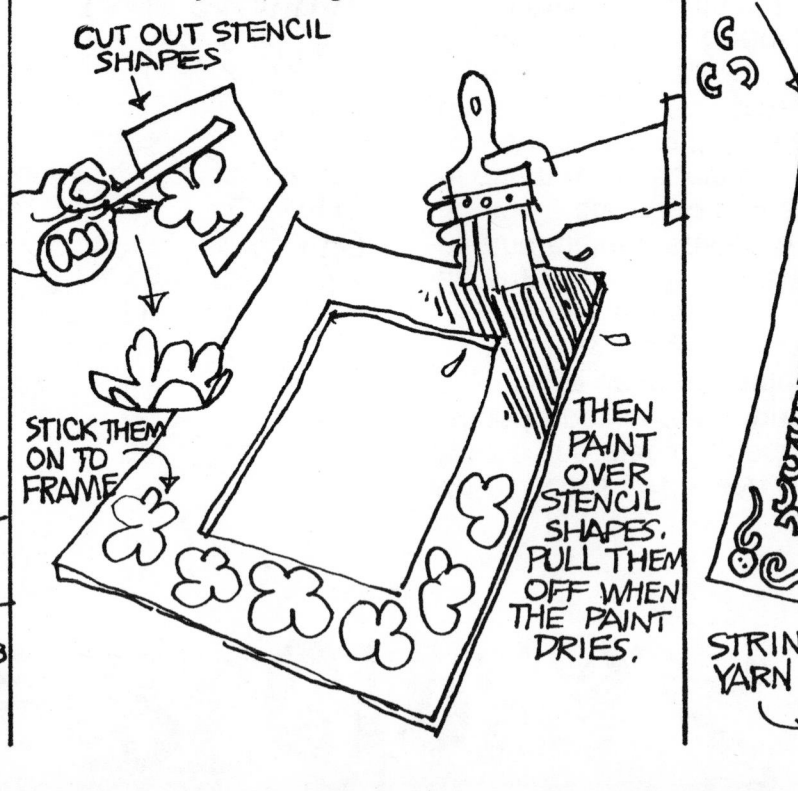

CUT OUT STENCIL SHAPES

STICK THEM ON TO FRAME

THEN PAINT OVER STENCIL SHAPES. PULL THEM OFF WHEN THE PAINT DRIES.

MACARONI

STRING OR YARN

BUTTONS OR BEADS

GLUE

Make a frame or border with a super personal touch by using clay block or art eraser prints for your design. Shape the clay into a square block. Press shapes and patterns into one side with sticks and other instruments. (You might work your initials into the design.) Then dip the block into a pan of paint and "print" your border or frame of paper or cloth.

Cut frames, mats, and borders from contact paper, wallpaper or fabric. Try using popsicle sticks, leaves, or a collage of magazine pictures trimmed to fit just perfectly!

MOLD A BLOCK OF CLAY WITH A CARVED SHAPE ON IT.

DIP CLAY DESIGN INTO A PAN OF PAINT & APPLY TO FRAME

TRIM OFF TO EDGE OF FRAME

WALLPAPER ROLL

MAGAZINE

THAT'S BERNY'S HAND REACHING IN THERE!

17

KEEPERS

For keeping your art treasures when you've run out of hanging space, create one of these folders for stashing things away.

POCKET FOLDER

Use a large sheet of cardboard. Fold about three inches over at each end to make pockets or flaps. Sew or staple the flaps at the top and bottom. Keep your paper tucked under each flap. (You may or may not want to fold your large cardboard like a book.) But DO add your own special decorative touches to the outside—perhaps a design that includes your name or initials.

FOLD DOWN AND STAPLE

BINDER FOLDER

Fold a large cardboard sheet in half. Punch two holes near the fold and string ribbon or yarn through the holes. Make matching holes in your papers and string them to the folder. Make a tab closure for your folder by cutting two slits in the cover as shown. Paste a cardboard strip tab to the back of the folder, bend over and feed it through the slits to close. Decorate the outside of your folder to suit your personality!

HUMONGOUS FOLDER

For oversize masterpieces, purchase a large cardboard art portfolio in an art or office supply store. Make wild, interesting designs on the outside and label it some outlandish sort of thing such as "Creations by a Brilliant Young Master" or "Fantasies of the Moon Mad."

BERNY'S MOST HUMONGOUSSED FOLDER

GET READY

broken lollipop pieces (all colors, transparent)

a variety of hard candies and jelly-based candies (no chocolates)

licorice strands (any flavors)

white glue or any glue that dries clear

pencil

posterboard or other stiff background material

Bible story picture books

oven (optional)

GET SET

1. Sketch lightly with your pencil on the background material a simple landscape which might have been the setting for a Bible story or event. (Bible story picture books may help you.) Here are some suggestions:

   Jesus' baptism

   The plains of the Jezreel Valley at sunset

   Shepherd's field at Bethlehem

   The hills of Judea

   Mount Hermon (Joshua 11)

   The valley of Aijalon where Joshua prayed for the sun and moon to stand still (Joshua 10)

   Ruins of Jericho

   The Garden of Eden

   The Garden of Gethsemane

2. Use broken lollipop pieces and other candies to create mosaic skies and lands. Fill in your sketched outline by laying each piece carefully in place. (If necessary, break or trim to fit.) When a section of the mosaic is neatly in place, glue each individual piece to the background with glue.

3. To create a very special effect, lay the finished mosaic in a moderate oven for a short time to allow the candies to melt slightly. Lay flat to cool. DO NOT EAT!

GO

Share your landscapes with friends and family, telling about the event that may have happened at the place you have chosen.

PATCHWORK SKIES & LICORICE LANDS

the CREATION CONNECTION

Creation story
Any landscape mentioned
in the Bible

21

GLOVE PUPPETS

GET READY
a glove, the size of your hand
  or a little bigger
felt-tip markers
scraps of cloth and paper, yarn,
  string, lace, trimmings, etc.
glue
needle and thread (optional)

GET SET
1. Choose a favorite Bible story that has three to five main characters.
2. Make each finger and the thumb of the glove into one of those characters by "dressing" it with scraps. (Be sure each one faces the palm side of the glove.)

GO
Put your hand in the glove and practice using your "puppets" to tell the story to the person in your mirror. Then tell it to your friends or classmates. (When you want a character to be "off-stage," just fold that finger down to your palm.)

SHADRACH

JESUS

MESHACH

KING

ABEDNEGO

the CREATION CONNECTION

Any story with three or more characters.

SEE-THRU PAINTINGS

How often do you stop to thank God for your wonderful world? Do you remember that hills and trees and soil and sand and clouds and skies and grass are all miracles of His creation? Does it amaze you that He made men and women smart enough to use His resources to build houses and stores and churches and skyscrapers, and make things like cars and roads and radio towers and swing sets and telephone poles? Give Him a gift of your time and your thoughtful thanksgiving as you do this special activity.

GET READY
a big glass window OR, if you want to work
    outside, a sheet of polyethylene stretched on
    a wooden frame
paints and brushes

GET SET
Stand a few feet away from your window and look through it at the world. As you do so, pretend you are looking at a large painting of what you see, rather than the real things.

GO
Now, paint that scene by outlining with paint and filling in the shapes and lines you see in the window. (Just trace the landscape with your brushes.) Try to match your colors to the real colors you see outside.

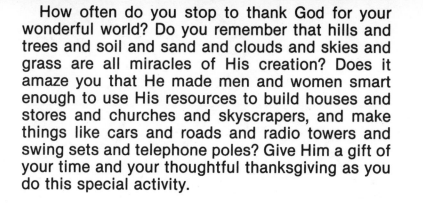

the CREATION CONNECTION
Awareness of natural beauty, creation
Awareness of material blessings,
Awareness of resources,
both natural and human
Conservation responsibility

23

Storybook Backgrounds

GET READY
an old wallpaper book
scissors
paste
crayons or felt-tip pens
several paper dolls
stapler, tape

GET SET
1. Tear from a wallpaper book six to eight pages which are rather plain or simple textured patterns. Bind them together in a booklet with stapler and tape.
2. Make the last page in your booklet a pocket page by cutting and taping (or stapling) a half page to the lower half of this page. Store several sets of paper dolls in this pocket page.
3. On the cover page, write the words STORYBOOK BACKGROUND by _____.
   your name
4. Use each remaining page in the book to create a background scene on which you can move your paper dolls to tell a favorite Bible story. Here are some suggestions for background scenes:
   (1) an indoor house scene
   (2) an outdoor yard scene
   (3) a water scene—by a lake or stream
   (4) a church scene
   (5) a street scene

GO
Carry your booklet to school, club meetings, baby-sitting jobs and other places where you can use it to tell Bible stories to other children OR use it to plan and enjoy stories that you like to do just for yourself.

the CREATION CONNECTION

Any set of Bible stories

GET READY

a cardboard box (just big enough for you to sit in)
2 large pieces of tagboard or cardboard
bright paints or felt-tip pens
glue or stapler
a small stool
a drinking straw
yarn or string
lightweight rope
an adult with a sharp knife or scissors

GET SET

1. Read or ask someone to read to you the story of Jehu, the wild chariot driver. The Lord told Elisha to make Jehu king of Israel and to send him to kill the whole household of Ahab and Jezebel. That is just what he did! (See 2 Kings 9.)

2. Ask an adult to help you cut your box into a chariot shape as shown.

3. Paint the outside of your chariot with bright colors in fancy designs.

4. Cut huge circles out of cardboard to make wheels for your chariot. Paint them a color to match your chariot.

5. Set your chariot box on a small stool. Now, attach a wheel to each side of your chariot. (Make them hang down over the side of the stool so they just touch the floor.)

6. When your chariot is ready, make yourself a whip by attaching yarn or string to the end of a drinking straw. (It will be fun to swing, but it won't hurt anyone.)

GO

Get someone to play "horse" for you. Put a long rope around the person's waist—then climb into your chariot. Sit on your knees and take the two ends of the rope in your hands like reins. Holler "YAHOO" and swing your whip. Pretend you are Jehu or a Charioteer in King Solomon's army.

HINTS: *If you can't find a person to be a "horse," you might use your stuffed animals as pretend horses! If you have a toy wagon, you may substitute the wagon for the stool. Then you will have a speedier chariot!*

A BOX CHARIOT

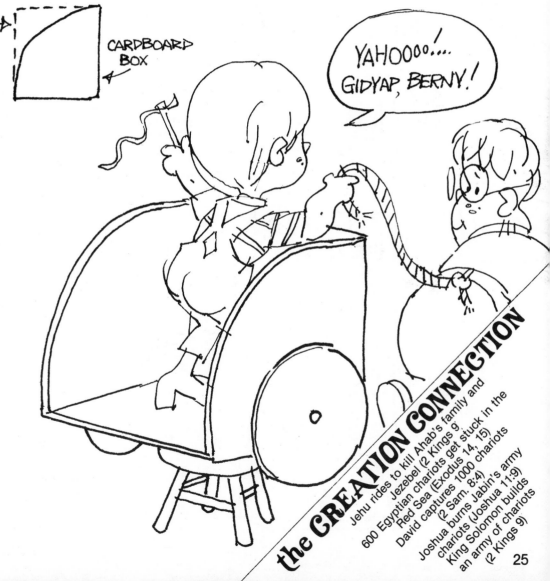

CUT AWAY THIS SIDE OF BOX ON A CURVE..

CARDBOARD BOX

YAHOOOO!.... GIDYAP, BERNY!

the CREATION CONNECTION

Jehu rides to kill Ahab's family and Jezebel (2 Kings 9)
600 Egyptian chariots get stuck in the Red Sea (Exodus 14, 15)
David captures 1000 chariots (2 Sam. 8:4)
Joshua burns Jabin's army chariots (Joshua 11:9)
King Solomon builds an army of chariots (2 Kings 9)

25

BIBLE BOOKENDS

GET READY
Two solid bricks OR four bricks with holes in center
enamel or acrylic paints
brushes
glue
felt fabric
scissors

GET SET
1. Clean bricks.
2. (For two bricks) Set bricks on small end.
   (For four bricks) Set each set of two bricks on widest surface and glue together.
3. Paint surfaces (as shown) with a design or picture of your choice and set to dry.
4. Cut felt fabric to fit the bottom surface of the brick. Glue in place to protect furniture.

GO
Use your finished bookends to keep your Bible, devotional books, and Bible school materials together on a shelf or table in your room. OR use the bookends as a gift to someone special.

Suggestions
angels
lion and lamb
Bibles
praying hands
rainbows
soldiers
flower and butterflies

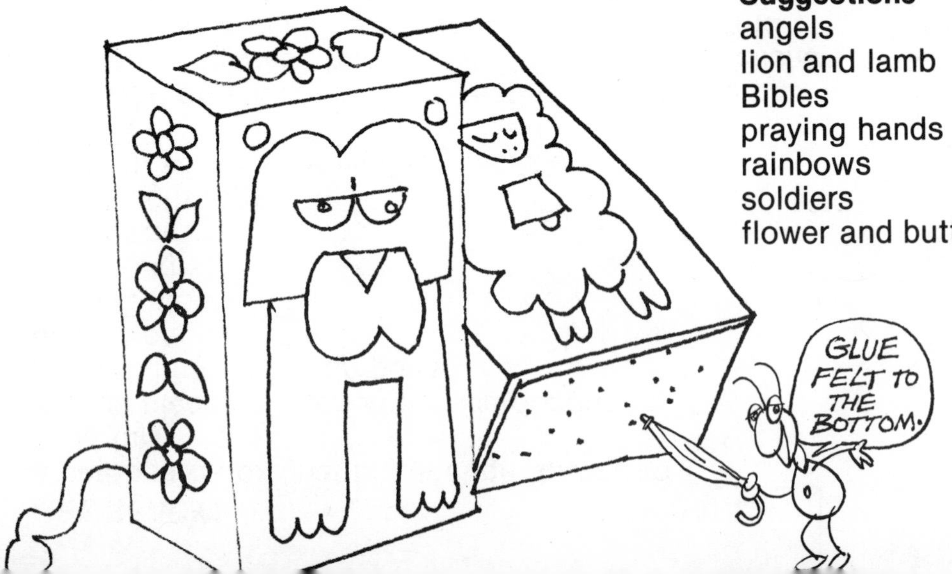

GLUE FELT TO THE BOTTOM.

the CREATION CONNECTION

Gift idea
General Craft Project

A BABY TO HOLD!

GET READY
an empty walnut shell
scraps of fabric, trim, and lace
cotton or polyester stuffing
tiny beads or buttons
a thumb cut off an old glove OR an old nylon
  stocking
glue, scissors, string
fine-point, felt-tip pen (permanent)

GET SET
1. Press some cotton into the nutshell and glue a
   piece of fabric over it to look like a tiny
   mattress.
2. Stuff the glove thumb with cotton OR cut a
   2-inch circle of nylon stocking and gather it
   around a ball of cotton. Tie at the bottom with
   string. This will be the baby's head.
3. Glue tiny buttons or beads to the head for
   eyes.
4. Use permanent marker to make mouth, nose,
   and rosy cheeks.
5. Add a few wisps of yarn for hair and use a
   piece of lace for a bonnet. Glue to the head.
6. Tuck the baby into the nutshell.
7. Cut a small piece of fabric for a blanket and
   tuck it into the shell, leaving only the baby's
   head showing.

GO
Rock the baby and sing a soft, quiet hymn or
lullaby.

the CREATION CONNECTION

Baby Moses
Baby Jesus
Loving care

SECRET SIGNS

The Christians of Bible times had a secret symbol which they used to identify themselves. It was a fish. The reason they chose a fish to represent their faith was probably because there were five Greek words which were especially important to Christians:

Jesus   Christ   God's   Son   Savior

The first Greek letter in each of these words spelled out the word *fish.* It was sort of like a code. Often, an early Christian artist would include some form of a fish in each drawing or painting he did ... a wood or tile designer would include a fish shape somewhere in his design to indicate that he was a Christian. In this activity, you will have an opportunity to do the same.

GET READY

any art medium (clay, wood or soap carving, paint, crayon, etc.)
tools to use with your chosen medium
pencil, paper

GET SET

Sketch on paper an artistic idea, picture, or design in which is hidden the symbol of the early Christians — a fish. Plan how you will create a product that shows your idea.

GO

Paint, sculpt, carve, or draw your idea. Show the finished product to friends and family and see if they can identify the secret symbol. Hang it where it will be a reminder to you of the early Christians and encourage your own Christian faith.

IF ANYONE CAN FIND A FISH IN THERE IT WILL BE ME

the CREATION CONNECTION

Early Christian symbols

TWO BY TWO

GET READY
animal-shaped cookie cutters
bread
sandwich spreads
the story of Noah's ark (Gen. 6:5-9:17)

GET SET
1. Lay out two pieces of bread for each friend you invite for lunch or a tea party.
2. Spread all the bread with peanut butter and jelly, ham salad, tuna salad, egg salad, or another favorite sandwich spread.
3. Let each friend choose one animal-shaped cookie cutter and use it to make a pair of open-face sandwich animals from Noah's story. (The cutters must be pressed firmly into the center of each piece of bread.)
4. Put each pair of animals on a paper plate and add some orange and apple slices, carrot and celery sticks. Pour each friend a glass of milk and seat everyone around a table.

GO
Before you eat, read the story of Noah from Genesis 6:5-9:17. Then say thank you to God for saving Noah, his family, and every living species ... and for these sandwiches! While you eat, see if you and your friends can answer these questions about Noah's story:
1. Why did God want to destroy the earth?
2. Why did God choose Noah as the man to make the ark?
3. God told Noah to take one pair of every animal, but to take seven pairs of some animals. Why?
4. How old was Noah when the flood came?
5. What was God's promise to Noah about the earth?
6. What did God say would be the reminder for this promise?
   (Answers in the Appendix of this book.)

P.S.
Don't throw away the bread crusts.
Eat them OR give them to an animal
to enjoy.

the CREATION CONNECTION
Noah's ark

Crumpled Paper Pictures

GET READY
chicken wire and a wood frame
 OR a chain link fence
several colors of tissue paper
 OR any paper that crumples easily

GET SET
1. Staple a piece of chicken wire to a wood frame OR do your project outside on a section of chain link fence.
2. Think of a scene from a favorite Bible story or choose an object that represents an idea from the Bible that you would like to share with friends and neighbors. (Large, simple objects are easiest to work with.)

GO
Use one color of tissue paper to outline each large object. Crumple pieces of tissue and stuff each piece into one hole of the fence. Then fill in the center of that object with the same color. Use a different color to outline and fill in each object. Fill all the remaining space around the object(s) with yet another color to create a background effect.

> **NOTE:** *You might invite lots of friends to help you! A huge area of fencing can be done with a large group of workers. Each person may do his own design OR the whole group may work together to create one big scene.*

BRACE THE FRAME ON THE BACK OF EACH CORNER.

the CREATION CONNECTION
A scene from any Bible story, rainbow, heart, Chrismon symbols, cross, etc.

BUTTONS, BROOMSTICKS & BUMPERSTICKERS

GET READY
the Book of Proverbs (from the Scripture)
a yellow highlighter pen AND a red pencil
plain contact paper
large safety pins
felt-tip pens
flat sticks or lattice wood strips
stapler
tape

GET SET
1. Read the entire Book of Proverbs. (The Living Bible paraphrase is suggested for easy understanding.) It is full of wonderful advice for kids and grownups alike. As you read, underline with a yellow marker every verse that is good for a kid to remember. Mark with red every verse that you think is especially good for the grownups in your house to remember.
2. Assemble all the materials you need to make buttons, poster-signs and bumper stickers: Use contact paper for bumper stickers; tagboard, safety pins, and tape for buttons; sticks, poster board, and staplers for poster-signs.
3. Choose the five Proverbs you think are most important for kids to remember and the three Proverbs you think are most important for grownups. Make a button, poster-sign, or bumper sticker for each. (When you finish, you should have eight Proverb reminders.)

GO
Wear them, give them to friends and parents, display them wherever you think people might see them and be reminded of things they should do or not do. Afterward, place the ones for kids in your room where they can be constant reminders of how you should conduct your life.

A WISE MAN THINKS AHEAD

A LAZY MAN SLEEPS SOUNDLY AND GET

WORK BRINGS PROFIT; TALK BRINGS POVERTY

FLYER

REVERENCE FOR GOD ADDS HOURS TO EACH DAY

JESUS LOVES YOU

TRUTH STANDS THE TEST OF TIME; LIES ARE EXPOSED

the CREATION CONNECTION

The Book of Proverbs

ROAR!
Says the LION

GET READY

orange or yellow construction
paper
brown or yellow yarn
scissors
glue
felt-tip pens
"Roar!" Says the Lion choral
reading

GET SET

1. Cut a lion's head shape (child's mask-size) like
   the one on this page from orange or yellow
   construction paper.
2. Use felt-tip pens to draw in eyes, nose,
   mouth, and whiskers.
3. Cut short lengths (about 2 inches) of yarn and
   glue around the entire edge of the lion's head.

GO

Read the poem below with a loud, exaggerated
voice. Make the lion r-r-r-roar! If you do this
activity with a whole group of children, the leader
should say the entire poem, and the others should
join in on just the underlined phrases.

ROAR! SAYS THE LION

"R-R-R-ROAR!" said the lion,
I'll rip and tear."
"R-R-R-ROAR!" said the lion,
But Daniel didn't scare.
He was God's man
And He could pray.
God locked the lion's jaws
And threw the key away!!

"R-R-R-ROAR!" said the lion.
I'll eat your sheep!"
"R-R-R-ROAR!" said the lion
But David didn't leap.
He knew the Lord
Was on his side,
So he fought that lion
'Til the lion died!

"R-R-R-ROAR!" says the lion.
He's the devil's disguise.
"R-R-R-ROAR!" says the lion,
"You're just the right size!
I'll get you if you
Come my way!"
"Go away old devil ...
With God I'll stay!"

the CREATION CONNECTION

Daniel in the Lions' Den (Daniel 6)
David Kills a Lion (I Sam. 17:34-37)
I Peter 5:8 (... The devil like a
roaring lion, walketh
about, seeking whom
he may
devour ..)

33

GET READY

A serving tray
plate
cup or glass
2 skewers OR 3-4 coffee
  stirrers OR toothpicks
fresh fruit, hard cheese
bread, butter
coffee, tea, milk, or juice
a flower or greens
a small card
ribbon or yarn
paper doily (optional)
napkin
crayons or felt-tip pens

GET SET

1. Prepare a breakfast tray for your special person. Use a paper doily to "fancy" up the tray OR make one by adding your own fancy design or flowers to the corners of an open paper napkin. Spread the napkin on the bottom of the tray.

2. Roll a folded napkin, corner to corner, and tie it with a ribbon or piece of bright yarn.

3. Make a simple menu of:
   buttered toast
   coffee, tea, or milk
   fruit and cheese kabobs
   (That's chunks of fresh fruit like apple, orange, banana, pineapple, melon, or strawberry, and hunks of hard yellow or white cheese, served on a stick.)

4. Add a flower ... or just a sprig of green (cut from a bush in the yard), tied with ribbon or yarn, AND a small card on which is written a favorite Scripture verse, proverb, love note, or thought for the day.

GO

Serve your tray quietly and cheerfully! Don't forget to smile and say, "I love you!"

P.S.   This is a good idea for a non-special day too — especially when someone has been feeling sad or neglected!

A SURPRISE BREAKFAST!

Everyone loves surprises — especially someone who is celebrating a special day such as a birthday, anniversary, or Mother's Day. (Gifts are expected later in the day, but not so early in the morning.) Be the first one to surprise the honoree!

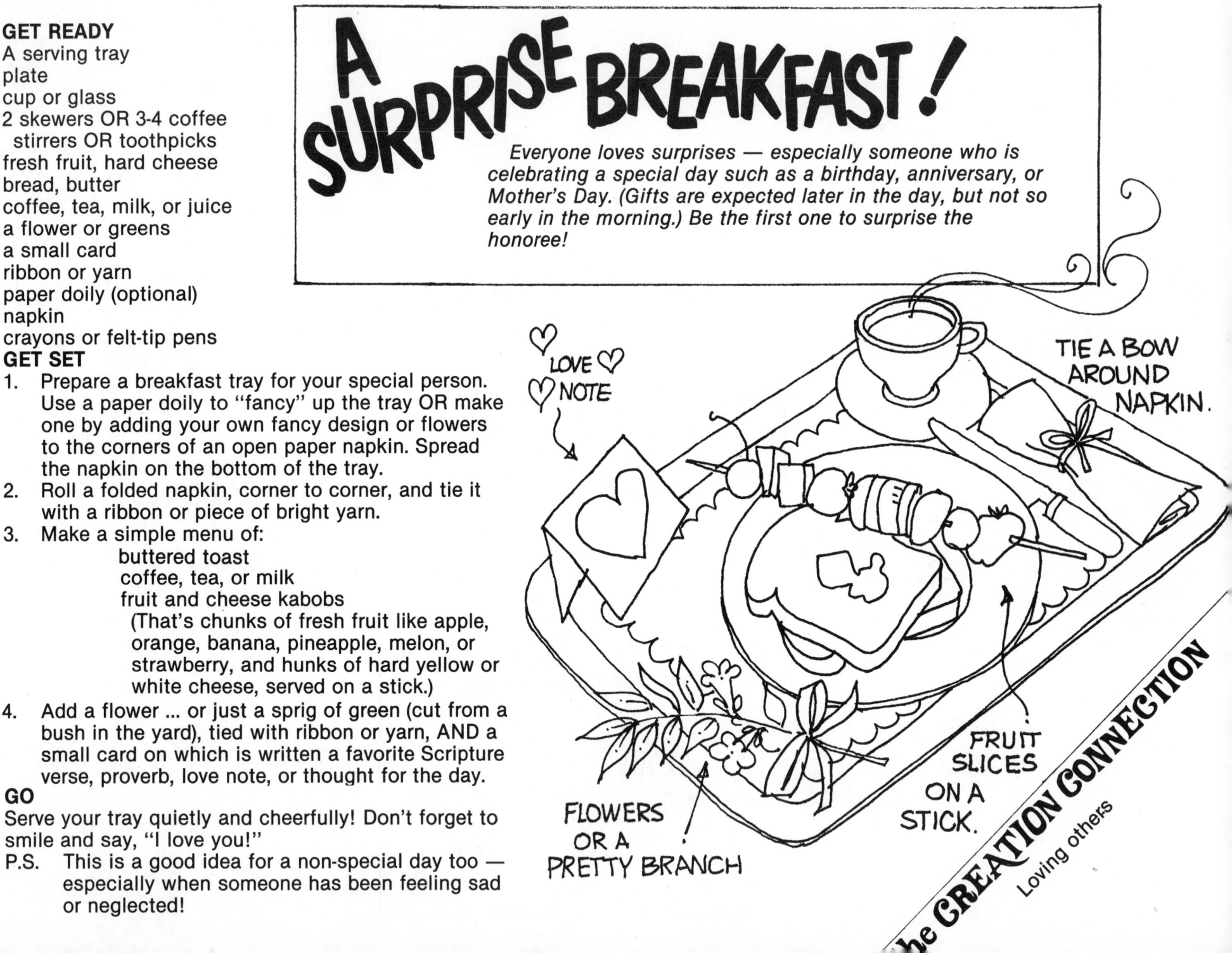

LOVE ♡ NOTE

TIE A BOW AROUND NAPKIN.

FRUIT SLICES ON A STICK.

FLOWERS OR A PRETTY BRANCH

The CREATION CONNECTION
Loving others

PLAY MASKS

GET READY
cardboard, tag or heavy
construction paper
large-size tongue depressors
pictures of the Bible characters
you want to create (optional)
paint or crayons
material and yarn scraps

GET SET
1. Choose a favorite Bible story.
2. Cut a head-size piece of heavy tag or construction paper for each character. (It may be round, square, or shaped like a head.)
3. Attach a tongue depressor to each "mask" for use as a handle.
4. Use pictures of the Bible characters to help you create the faces and special identities of each person.
5. Color each mask and use scraps to add hair, beard, eyeglasses, headwear, etc.

GO
Tell your favorite Bible story, using the masks in much the same way as you would use puppets, acting out each character as he appears in the story. Hold the proper mask in front of your face and change your voice for each character. You can do a one-man show, or you may offer your friends a mask or two each and invite them to join with you!

the CREATION CONNECTION

Any Bible story

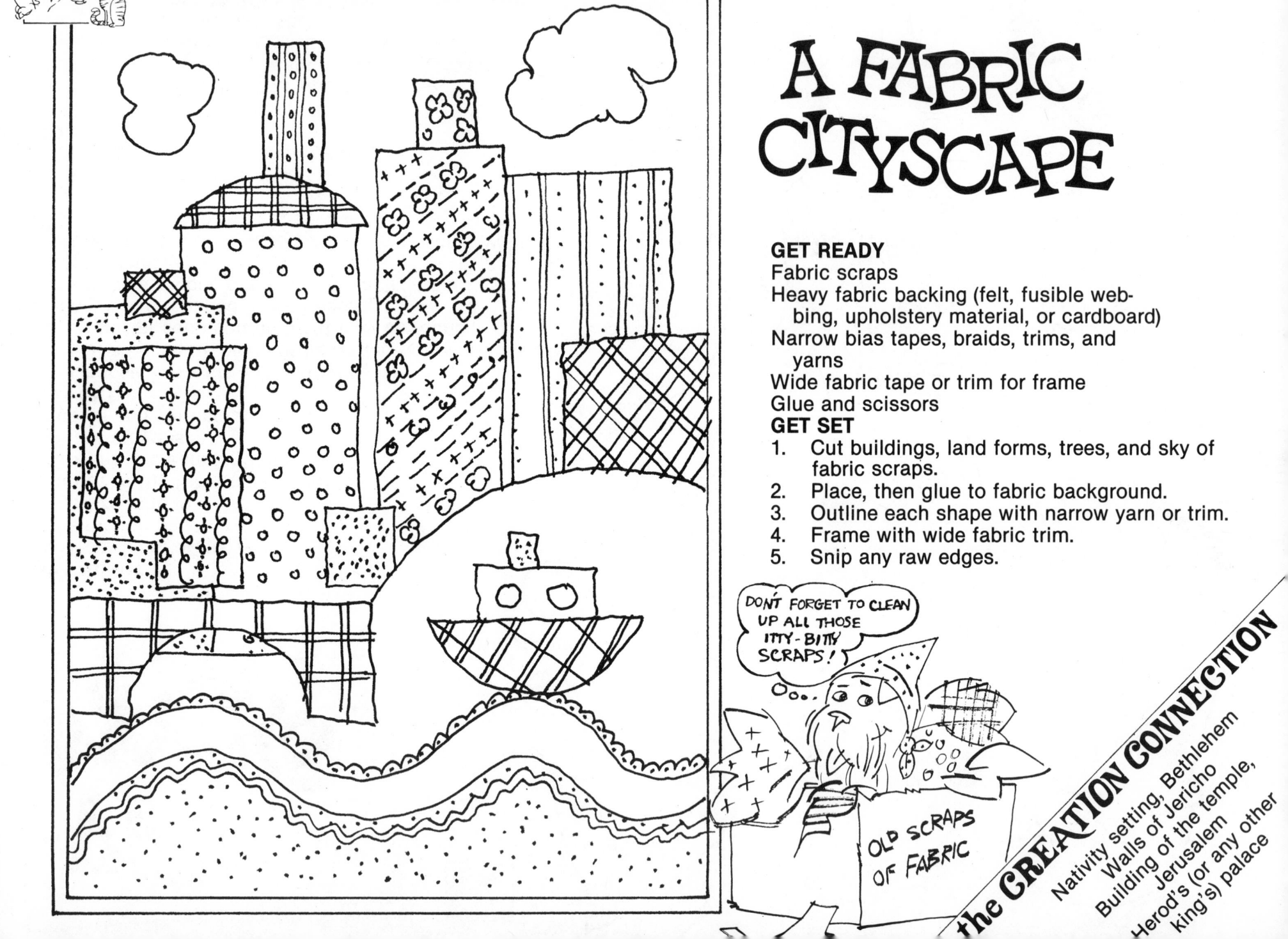

A FABRIC CITYSCAPE

GET READY

Fabric scraps

Heavy fabric backing (felt, fusible web-
bing, upholstery material, or cardboard)

Narrow bias tapes, braids, trims, and
yarns

Wide fabric tape or trim for frame

Glue and scissors

GET SET

1. Cut buildings, land forms, trees, and sky of fabric scraps.
2. Place, then glue to fabric background.
3. Outline each shape with narrow yarn or trim.
4. Frame with wide fabric trim.
5. Snip any raw edges.

DON'T FORGET TO CLEAN UP ALL THOSE ITTY-BITTY SCRAPS!

OLD SCRAPS OF FABRIC

the CREATION CONNECTION

Nativity setting, Bethlehem

Walls of Jericho

Building of the temple, Jerusalem

Herod's (or any other king's) palace

WHY GO TO CHURCH?

_____ Because God says so!

_____ To learn

_____ To have fun and fellowship with Christian friends

_____ Because it's good discipline to make a commitment to be there every week and take part.

_____ To support other Christian brothers and sisters.

_____ To show the world that spiritual things are important to you.

_____ To be part of a group that can have some good influence in our world.

_____ To worship as a group of believers rather than just alone.

_____ To develop useful skills and talents.

_____ To gain opportunities for Christian responsibility and service.

_____

_____

GET READY

paper, pencil, a Bible, a good head

GET SET

1. Here are some reasons for going to church. Consider each one carefully. Cross out any you do not agree with. Write in any additional reasons you can think of.

2. Now, in the blank beside the ONE reason you think is MOST important, write the number 1. Beside the reason you think is next in importance, write the number 2, and so on until all reasons are numbered.

3. Make a survey of Christian friends and acquaintances — both adults and kids. Do not show your list of reasons, but ask each of them to give you three reasons why they go to church. Write down their answers.

GO

Compare their answers with your list of reasons. Do they feel pretty much like you do about church attendance? Think about the differences between their ideas and yours. Then use a Bible concordance and try to find as many verses as possible that talk about believers worshipping together. See what God has to say about it. Share all your findings with your Sunday school class.

A SHEPHERD'S STAFF

GET READY

A sturdy, knobby branch or limb of a tree, about the height your shoulder (Be sure the tree is done with it!)

NOTE: *A shepherd's staff would have a curve at one end.*
A walking stick would be quite straight.

A dull knife or spatula

Brightly-colored, permanent felt-tip pens

GET SET

1. Shepherds and other Bible-times people who had to walk long distances often carried sticks to help them. Think of all the ways in which a walking stick could be helpful.
   Did you think of these? (Reaching, herding animals, protection, leaning on, measuring, or just something to be your very own ... that you can depend on ... like a friend.)

2. Make your own dependable walking stick by getting a piece of tree branch or limb. (It is more interesting if it has knobs and bumps on it.)

3. Scrape it bare with a dull knife or the edge of a spatula so it is smooth to touch. (This is hard work and will take a long time.)

4. Let the natural lines and lumps of the stick suggest interesting patterns for coloring your stick with permanent felt-tip pens.

GO

Make friends with your stick as you work ... Talk to it. Keep it in your room. Use it whenever you go for long walks.

COCKERPOOS MAKE GREAT SHEEP DOGS!

the CREATION CONNECTION

Any story in which Bible characters walked long distances or in which shepherds are major figures.

THE WALLS CAME TUMBLING DOWN!

GET READY
a tiny, thick pad of paper
pencil, crayons or felt-tip pens

GET SET
1. Begin with the last page of your pad of paper. Draw a simple picture of the Jericho wall on the lower right-hand part of the page.
2. On the next page (working backwards toward the front of your pad), draw the SAME pictures with a slight change.
3. Keep drawing the SAME PICTURE in the SAME SPOT on each page, changing it slightly each time until the top picture shows the wall all fallen down in crumbles.

GO
Hold the pad in one hand. Put your thumb under the back page and flip the pages . . . Watch the walls come tumbling down!

the CREATION CONNECTION
Sick man being let down through roof
Naaman dipping seven times
Jairus' daughter
Lazarus raised
Fall of Jericho

39

Some folks think that God sometimes moves and speaks in the winds. One thing of which we can be sure is that He alone controls the winds. Man cannot change the weather. This activity will make you more aware of God's winds.

WIND CHIMES

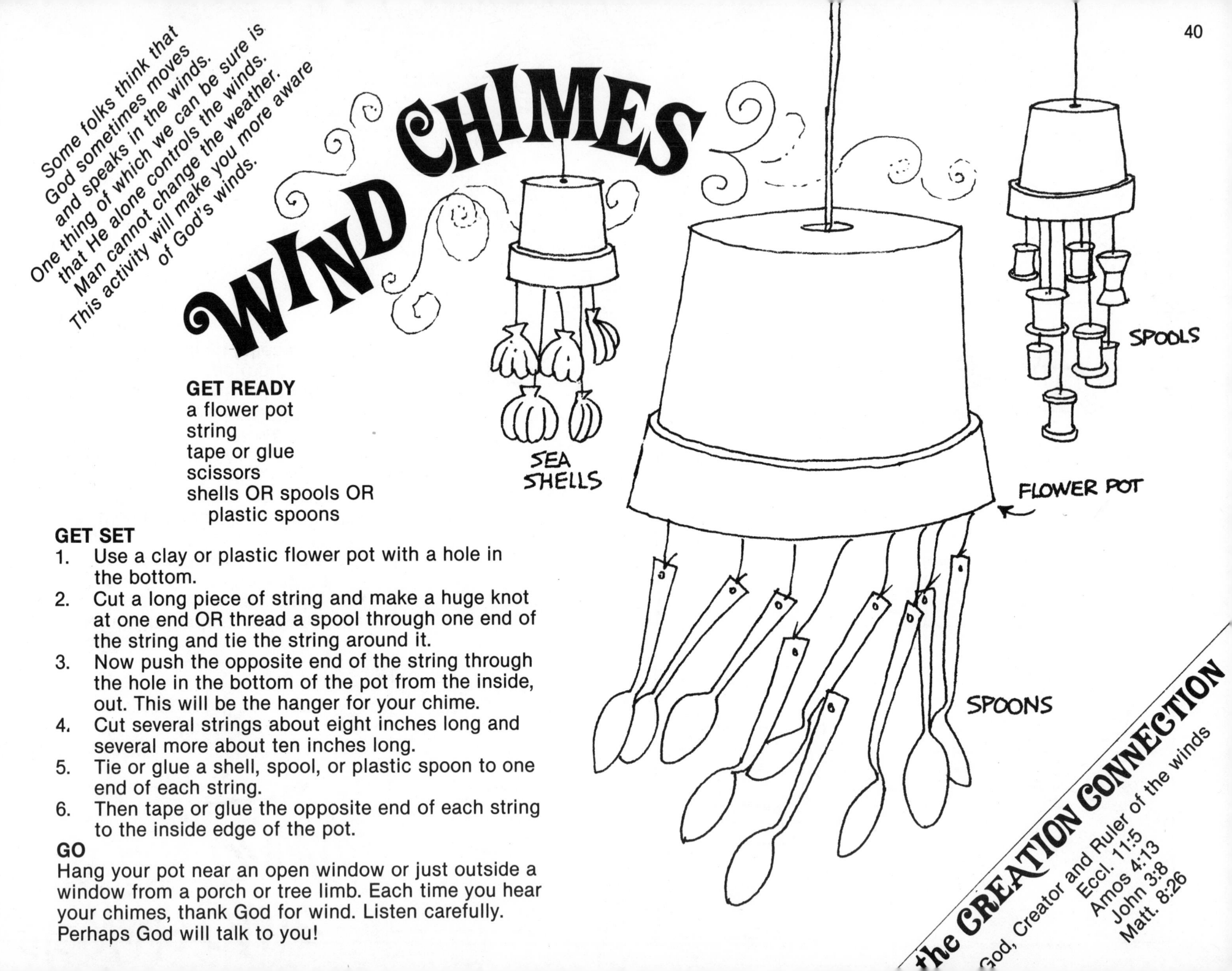

SEA SHELLS

SPOOLS

FLOWER POT

SPOONS

GET READY
a flower pot
string
tape or glue
scissors
shells OR spools OR
plastic spoons

GET SET
1. Use a clay or plastic flower pot with a hole in the bottom.
2. Cut a long piece of string and make a huge knot at one end OR thread a spool through one end of the string and tie the string around it.
3. Now push the opposite end of the string through the hole in the bottom of the pot from the inside, out. This will be the hanger for your chime.
4. Cut several strings about eight inches long and several more about ten inches long.
5. Tie or glue a shell, spool, or plastic spoon to one end of each string.
6. Then tape or glue the opposite end of each string to the inside edge of the pot.

GO
Hang your pot near an open window or just outside a window from a porch or tree limb. Each time you hear your chimes, thank God for wind. Listen carefully. Perhaps God will talk to you!

the CREATION CONNECTION
God, Creator and Ruler of the winds
Eccl. 11:5
Amos 4:13
John 3:8
Matt. 8:26

Make a Joyful NOISE!

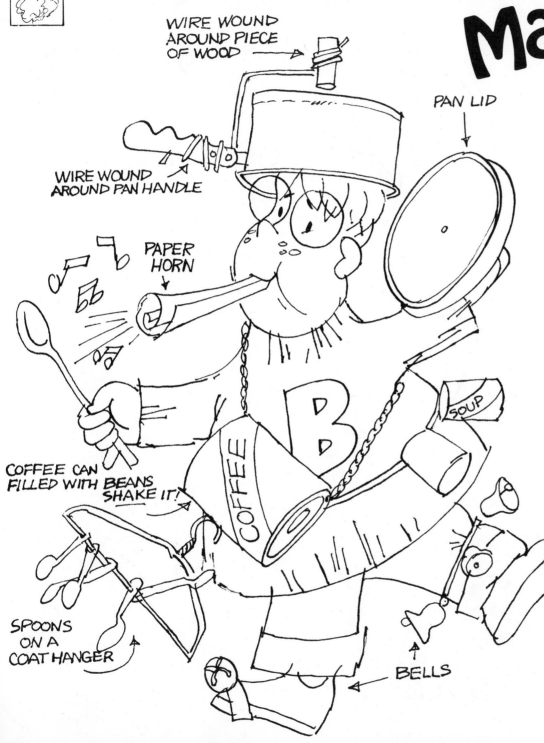

WIRE WOUND AROUND PIECE OF WOOD →

PAN LID

WIRE WOUND AROUND PAN HANDLE

PAPER HORN

COFFEE CAN FILLED WITH BEANS SHAKE IT!

SPOONS ON A COAT HANGER

SOUP

COFFEE

B

BELLS

GET READY
cardboard tubes
coffee cans
small bells
juice cans with beans or small
  stones
spoons, pot and pan lids
masking tape, string, and rope
old coat hangers or wire

GET SET
1. Collect all kinds of stuff like the things listed here to make rhythm band instruments.
2. Make as many as you can.

GO
Now, use tape, string, and wire to attach as many of these "instruments" as possible to your body so that you can become a one-man band ... playing and singing to your own accompaniment. Sing a loud and joyful song of praise!

the CREATION CONNECTION

Psalm 150

ERASABLE PICTURES

ZIPLOC BAG

I. "Paint-in-a-Bag"

GET READY
A Zip-loc plastic bag
Thick tempera or finger paint

GET SET
1. Mix paint and pour into a Zip-loc bag. (Fill only about one-fourth of the bag with paint. Press as much air as possible out of the bag; then close the bag securely.

GO
2. Use your finger to "draw" letters, numbers, and picture stories on the outside of your bag. Erase simply by rubbing the palm of your hand over the bag to smooth paint.

the CREATION CONNECTION

Reinforcing any Bible word or phrase associated with any Bible story

Use to write Bible Quiz answers pictures

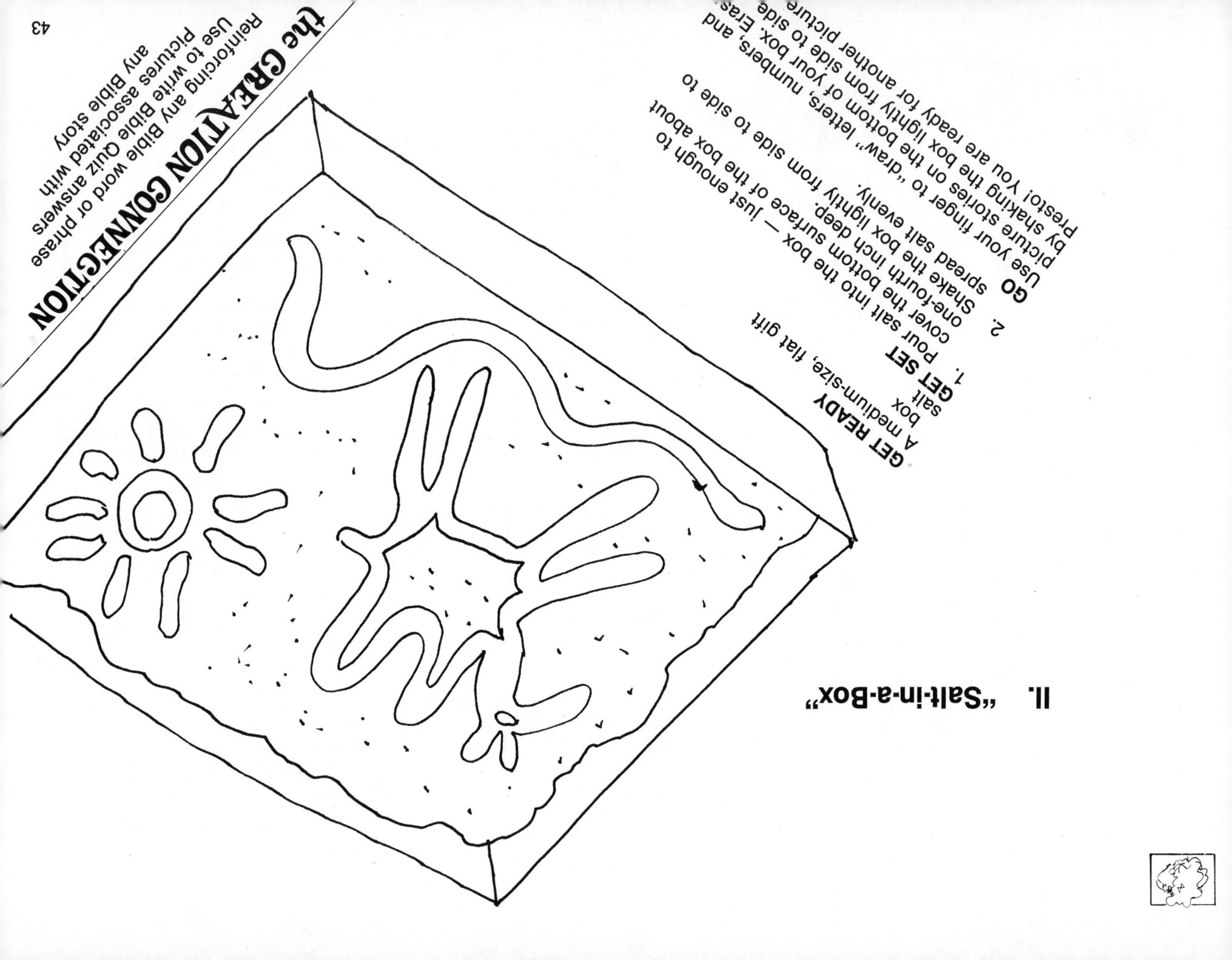

II. "Salt-in-a-Box"

GET READY
A medium-size, flat gift box
salt

GET SET
1. Pour salt into the box to cover the bottom surface of the box about one-fourth inch deep — just enough to
2. Shake the box lightly from side to side to spread the salt evenly.

GO
Use your finger to "draw" picture stories on the bottom of your box. Erase by shaking the box lightly from side to side, and presto! You are ready for another picture.

MARVELOUS MACHINE

GET READY

large-size mural paper—
as long as you are tall
crayons or paint
felt-tip markers
scissors
masking tape

GET SET

1. Lie down on the paper.
2. Ask someone to trace around your body.
3. Cut carefully on the lines.
4. Paint or color in clothes and features.
5. On the back side, label each body part with as many action words as you can think of that will describe what that part of your marvelous body can do!
6. Use masking tape to "seat" your paper self in a chair in your room.

GO

Introduce "yourself" to your friends and share all your action words. Maybe they can think of some words you have forgotten!

NOTE:

If you are familiar with the song "Marvelous Machine" by Huff, Gaither, and MacKenzie, this would be a good time to sing it.

the CREATION CONNECTION

Psalm 139:1-18, 23-24

STORM IN A JAR

SORT OF A HOME MADE "TELEVISION" SET!

GET READY
a small glass (baby food)
  jar with screw-on lid
modeling clay
waterproof felt pen
waterproof glue
cold, boiled water
crushed eggshell
glitter (optional)
miniature plastic figures,
  flowers, animals, creche
  scene, etc.

GET SET
1. Set tiny plastic figures in a small mound of clay, pressed into the lid of the jar.
2. Glue in both clay and figures and let dry thoroughly.
3. Fill jar almost to the top with water.
4. Add one heaping tablespoon of crushed eggshells and a pinch of glitter (optional) to the water.
5. Drip a ring of glue around inside edge of lid. Let it dry partially, then screw lid tightly on jar.

GO
When the glue has had time to dry, turn jar upside down and shake up a storm!

the CREATION CONNECTION
Winter (Use trees or snowman)
Gift idea
Christmas (Use plastic holly
  or miniature nativity)
Camel in desert
Ship at sea

Your Autograph Please!

GET READY
scrap lumber
sand paper
quick-drying spray paint OR
  glossy enamel and brush
permanent felt-tip pen(s)
list of required signatures
 (on this page — you may add
 to this list if you wish)
scrap paper and pencil

GET SET
1. Use a piece of scrap lumber to create a special autograph board. It can be any shape or size you wish.
2. Sand the board to make it smooth and save yourself the pain of splinters!
3. Paint the board a bright color and decorate it to your liking. Let it dry thoroughly.
4. Copy the required list of signatures on a small piece of paper and paste on the bottom side of the board.

GO
Invite the people listed on the bottom side of your board to sign autographs. Be sure they use a permanent felt-tip pen. Ask each one to include with his signature the reference for his favorite Bible verse. When you have collected all the autographs, place your board in a special place in your room. Look up one Scripture reference each day during your personal devotional time.

1. Your Sunday school teacher
2. A person who can recite all the books of the Bible accurately
3. An especially friendly person
4. A person who has known the Lord more than thirty years
5. Your pastor
6. A person who has known the Lord less than one year
7. Someone who can say John 3:16
8. A gospel songwriter
9. A person whose smile is special
10. Someone who can tell you how a person can be saved from his sin
11. Someone who can sing "This Little Light of Mine"
12. Someone who can quote a Scripture promise
13. Someone who loves you
14. Someone who is always doing nice things for others
15. Someone you don't know very well, but would like to know better
16. Someone you would like to grow up to be just like

A FRIEND MUST SHOW HIMSELF FRIENDLY

Aunt Marge
Prov. 20:11

Mom
Eph. 6:1

Dudely Dunty
JOHN 11:12

Joe Shamael
JOB 11:2

Cindy Schartz
Jimmy
James 4:8

Rusty Flint
JOHN 3:16

LUKE 3:6

Al Smith
JOHN 6:35

Fanny Fuddle
PSA. 111:4

Beth
PSA. 119:9

the CREATION CONNECTION
Looking up Scripture references
Interaction with other Christians

47

BAD NEWS GOOD NEWS

GET READY
A large piece of poster board
Construction paper—black and
  yellow, red and white
scissors, paste, pencil
felt-tip pen

GET SET
1. Measure the width of your poster to find the exact middle.
2. Draw a faint pencil line down the middle.
3. Now cover the left half of the poster with black construction paper and the right half with yellow.
4. At the top of the black half, write these words with letters cut from white construction paper:
   BAD NEWS
   At the top of the yellow half, use red construction paper letters to write GOOD NEWS
5. Then on the black half, place the words of Romans 3:23. Write the words with black pen on white strips of paper and paste them neatly in place.
6. Follow the same procedure, using red pen on white paper strips to write the words of Romans 3:24, and paste them on the yellow side of your poster.

GO
Read the poster's good and bad news to yourself and think about the meaning. Use your poster to share the news with your friends and family. Put it in your room on a wall or door where it will remind you to rejoice that Jesus canceled out the bad news and made the good news possible by his death on the cross.

the CREATION CONNECTION

Romans 3:23-24

JACOB'S WELL

In the years that Jesus lived on earth, the well was a very important part of every community. It was the place from which every family got nearly all the water they used. Sometimes people talked about important things when they met each other by the well. Read John 4:1-26 to learn about a very important conversation Jesus had at a well. That well still exists today in a little town in the country of Israel.

GET READY

a ½-pint milk carton
scissors or knife
2 drinking straws
tape
string
a ketchup cup (or substitute to use as a tiny pail)
tempera paint mixed with detergent
brush
glue

GET SET

1. Cut a small milk carton as shown. (Glue or staple the top shut if necessary.)
2. Use the top piece for the roof of the well, the bottom piece for the well shaft.
3. Cut 4 pieces of drinking straw and use tape or glue to attach one to each of the four inside corners of the base of the well to support the roof.
4. Poke a hole in two opposite sides of the roof and insert a long piece of straw.
5. Tape a string to the straw and turn the straw until the string is wound around it.
6. Now use string to attach a ketchup cup or other small "bucket-like" object to the wound string.

GO

Practice lowering your bucket into the well and bringing it back up again. You might even put some real water in your well!

① ② ③ ④

the CREATION CONNECTION

Jesus and the Samaritan woman at the well
Rebecca at the well

LOOK 'N LISTEN

GET READY
a Bible
a Bible storybook
paper and crayons
large envelopes
cassette tapes
tape recorder

GET SET
1. Decide on two or three special Bible stories that you would like to include in your Look 'n Listen Series. Read those stories in a Bible storybook and then again in your Bible to refresh your memory about all the details of the stories.
2. Prepare each story in the following manner:
   - Rewrite the story in your own words, making it exciting and especially interesting for young children.
   - Read your story aloud with marvelous, exaggerated expression and record on cassette tape.
   - Draw one or more good illustrations to accompany your story.
   - Place in a large envelope your written story, the tape-cassette of that story, and its accompanying illustrations.
   - Label the envelope with the name of the story.

GO
Now you have a lending library for your very own Look 'n Listen Series. Offer the cassettes to young children you know or lend them to the church library so that children may enjoy them at home or in their Sunday school classes.

the CREATION CONNECTION
Any Bible story for children

Have you ever tried to imagine what the world would be like without color? God not only made things that grow and work — he made them beautiful. This experiment will help you understand a little bit more about the qualities of color.

the Amazing Color Race

GET READY

a tall glass jar with a lid
3 strips cut from paper towel
3 paper clips
tape
red, green, and purple food coloring OR ink in these
  colors

GET SET

1. Put a little water in the bottom of a tall jar.
2. Cut three strips of paper towel, just taller than the jar and attach a paper clip to one end of each.
3. Put a fat dot of green ink or food coloring on one strip. On another strip, put a dot of red, and on the third, a dot of purple. The dots should be about one-half inch above the paper clips.
4. Hang the strips of paper in the jar so that the paper clips just touch the water. Tape the top ends to the jar and place the lid on the jar.

GO

Watch the water move up the strips of paper. What happens to the colors in the dots? If you watch carefully, you will see that some dots are made of more than one color. The colors in those dots will separate. One color will "outrun" the other toward the top of the jar and the other will "catch up" and rejoin the first color toward the end of the race. Which colors were the fastest? Isn't it intriguing to see how God has made colors? Thank God for color!

PAPER STRIPS

PAPER CLIPS

JAR

WATER

WOW! THE COLORS ARE RACING EACH OTHER. THIS IS NEAT!!

the CREATION CONNECTION

Thank God for colors

51

ANIMAL CRACKER ARK

FOLDED SHEET OF CONST. PAPER

TAPE CORNER

CUT

FOLD

GET READY

a box of animal crackers
2 pieces of construction paper
scissors
paste or tape
the story of Noah's ark (Genesis 6-9)

GET SET

1. Make a box of animal crackers into an ark! Cut one piece of construction paper just a bit longer and about 2" wider than the box. Fold the paper lengthwise and make it into a roof by taping or gluing it along the top edges of the box.
2. Cut a "door" in the side of the box as shown in the pictures and fold it down like a ramp.
3. Glue the box into the center of another piece of construction paper. Make a diagonal cut at each corner and fold up the edges to complete the ark.

GO

Ask someone to read the story of Noah's ark aloud from Genesis or from a Bible story book while you work on your ark. After the story, have an elephant or tiger or a bear for a snack!

the CREATION CONNECTION

Noah's ark

MITTEN FISH

GET READY
an old mitten
felt scraps
white glue
2 large buttons

GET SET
1. Use the picture as a guide.
2. Cut felt scraps to make teeth, fins and tail. Glue them to the body of the fish.
3. Glue or sew the buttons to each side for eyes.

GO
Put your hand inside the mitten and make your fish swim, dive, bite, nibble, and scare!

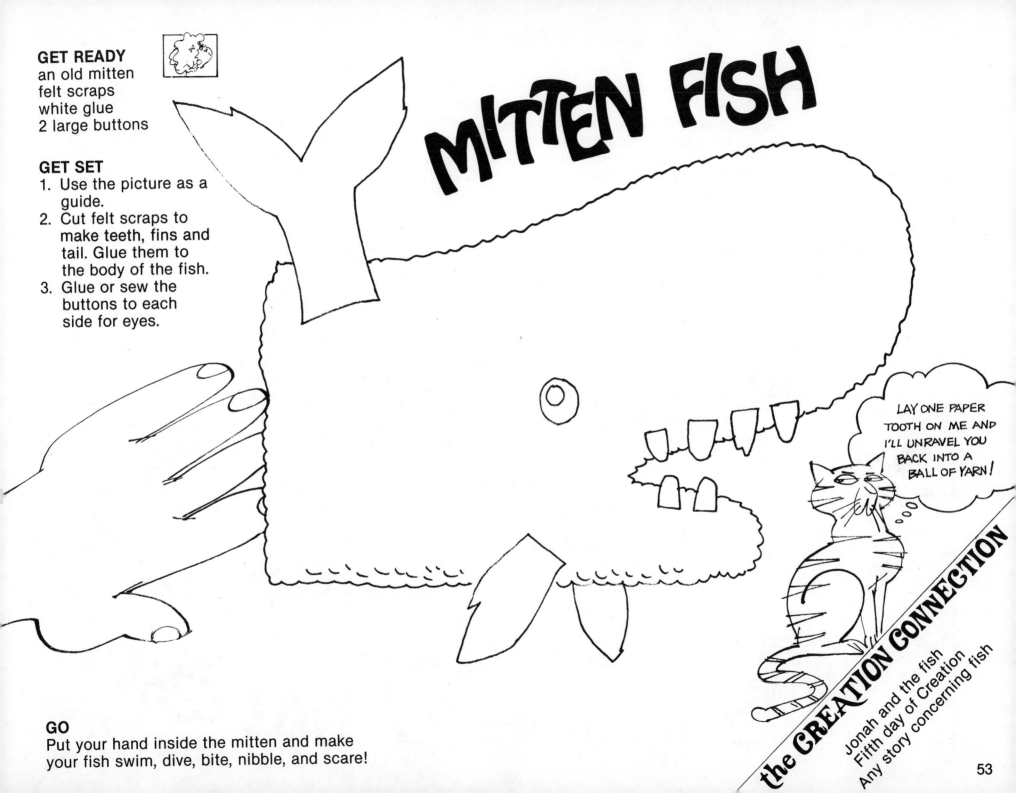

LAY ONE PAPER TOOTH ON ME AND I'LL UNRAVEL YOU BACK INTO A BALL OF YARN!

the CREATION CONNECTION
Jonah and the fish
Fifth day of Creation
Any story concerning fish

53

PAPER TREE!

GET READY
2 sheets of newspaper
tape
scissors
paint

GET SET

1. Lay out the sheets of newspaper
and roll them up.
Fasten the edge with transparent
tape at one end as shown.

2. Make four cuts about six inches
long in the other end.

PULL UP

3. Reach inside and gently pull the
insides up and out.
Spray or paint the finished tree.

GO
Make lots of trees to create a forest or jungle.
Use your tree(s) to illustrate a story like
Adam and Eve in the Garden, or Zaccheus.
"Plant" your tree in a box filled with sand
or stuffed paper.

the CREATION CONNECTION
Any Bible story or setting
that includes trees
Creation
Growing Things
Spring

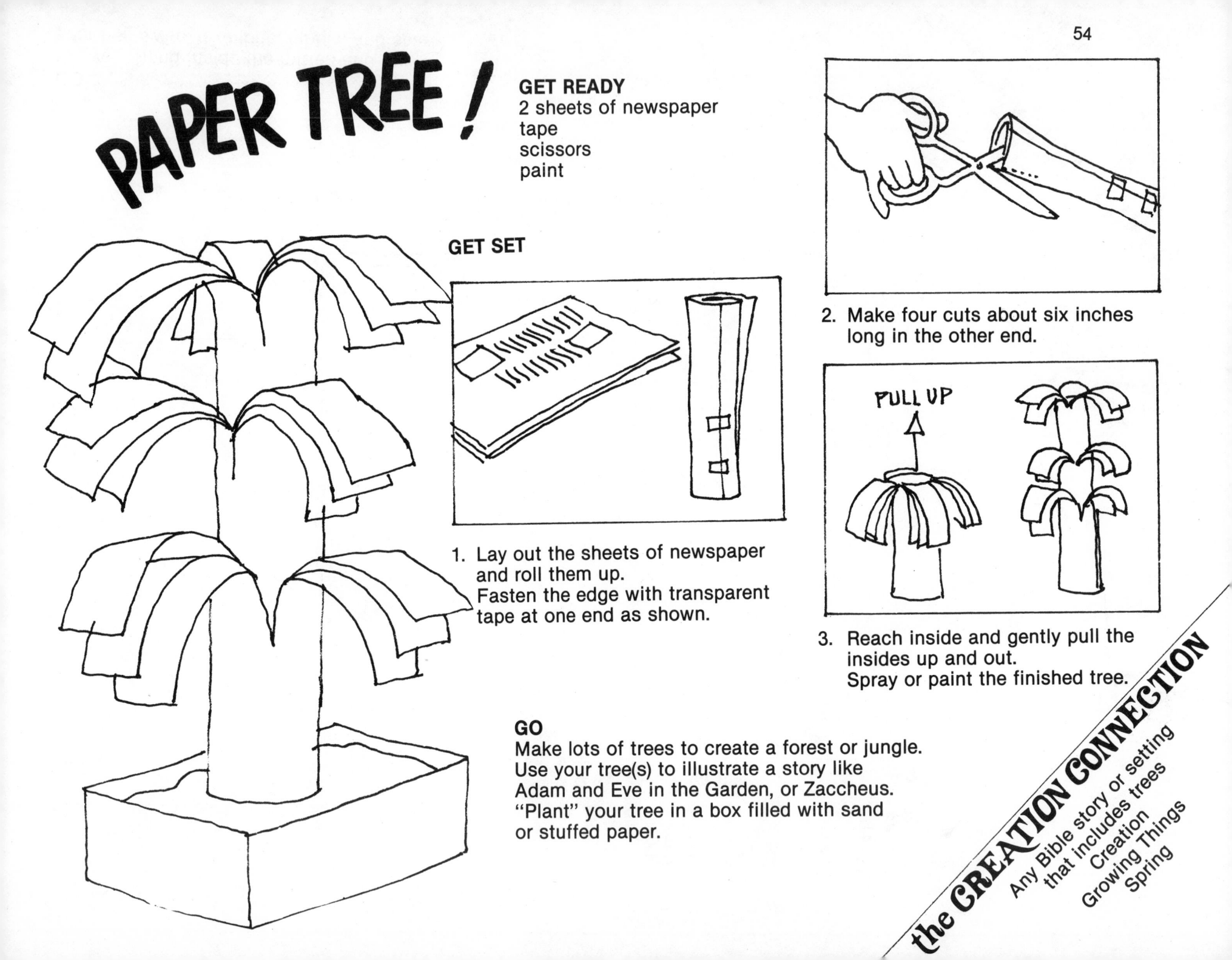

Birds 'n Butterflies

GET READY
a small, flat box
acetate (see-through plastic)
scissors
cellophane tape
tissue paper

GET SET
1. Use these patterns to cut bird and butterfly shapes from tissue.
2. Twist each one in the middle.
3. Cut acetate to fit over the box like a cover.
4. Place birds and butterflies in the box.
5. Tape acetate over the box.

GO
Rub the acetate and watch the birds and butterflies fly!

NOTE: *For younger children, prepare boxes and draw patterns on small folded pieces of tissue. Assist child in cutting and twisting birds and butterflies and help him tape acetate on box.*

WHEN I HOLD MY HAND OVER THE BOX, THE BUTTERFLIES 'N BIRDS... JUMP *UP!*

the CREATION CONNECTION

Creation
Spring

SCRIPTURE SCAVENGER HUNT

GET READY
paper and pencil
a King James version of the Bible for each participant
list of clues
large grocery bag for each participant

GET SET
1. Ask some friends or classmates to join you for a scavenger hunt.
2. Choose from the list of clues and Bible references on this page or use your own clues to create a list of objects to be found by the "hunters."

GO
1. Give each hunter the same list of "clues" and a King James version of the Bible.
2. At the GO signal, the "hunters" must look up each Bible reference to find the name of an object that can be obtained in the neighborhood.
3. When they have figured out from their Bible references what objects are to be found, they may work individually or in groups to collect all the objects. (Give them a time limit.)
4. The person or team who has gathered the most objects when the time is up wins the "hunt."

SOME CLUES TO USE
Give only the Bible references. The words in parentheses are the clues which the "hunters" must find. Keep those answers to check the bags of "bounty" as the "hunters" return.

John 15:6 (branch)
Exodus 13:6 (bread)
Genesis 21:19 (a bottle)
Judges 6:38 (a bowl)
Job 18:6 (a candle)
Exodus 20:6 (a commandment)
Psalm 72:16 (corn)
Amos 4:2 (a fish hook)
Jonah 1:17 (a fish)
Leviticus 13:39 (a freckled spot)
Isaiah 40:6 (a flower)
Leviticus 19:10 or Isaiah 18:5 (a grape)
Mark 1:6 (a girdle)
I Corinthians 11:25 (a cup)
II Timothy 1:5 (a grandmother)
Judges 5:26 or Jeremiah 23:29 (a hammer)
Isaiah 22:22 (a key)
Habakkuk 3:19 (a stringed instrument)
Matthew 20:10 (a penny)
Genesis 42:25 (a sack
Deuteronomy 25:9 (a shoe)
Mark 11:14 (fruit)
Job 24:20 (worm)
Psalm 64:7 or Zechariah 9:14 (an arrow)

According to Lev. 13:39 I gotta look for a GRAPE!

According to Jonah 1:17 I gotta look for a FISH!

I'll go with Jonah 1:17.... It's my favorite VERSE!

the CREATION CONNECTION

Bible reference drill

FACE IT!

GET READY
old magazines
scissors
paste
pens, pencils, crayons
white or light-colored construction
  paper

GET SET
1. Browse through several old magazines. Look
   for faces (JUST FACES ... disregard bodies,
   clothing, etc.) that remind you of Bible
   characters you have read about.
2. Cut out the faces and paste them on
   construction paper. Leave plenty of space
   around each face.
3. Now, use your pen, pencil, and crayons to
   create appropriate body, hair, clothing, etc. to
   fit the Bible character whose face you have
   chosen. Write the name of each character
   upside down at the bottom or on the back of
   the page.

GO
Share your newly-created Bible characters with
your friends. See if they can correctly identify
each one.

GLUE

GOODHOUSEKEEPING

the CREATION CONNECTION
Identifying outstanding features
and characteristics of
familiar Bible figures.

PALACES

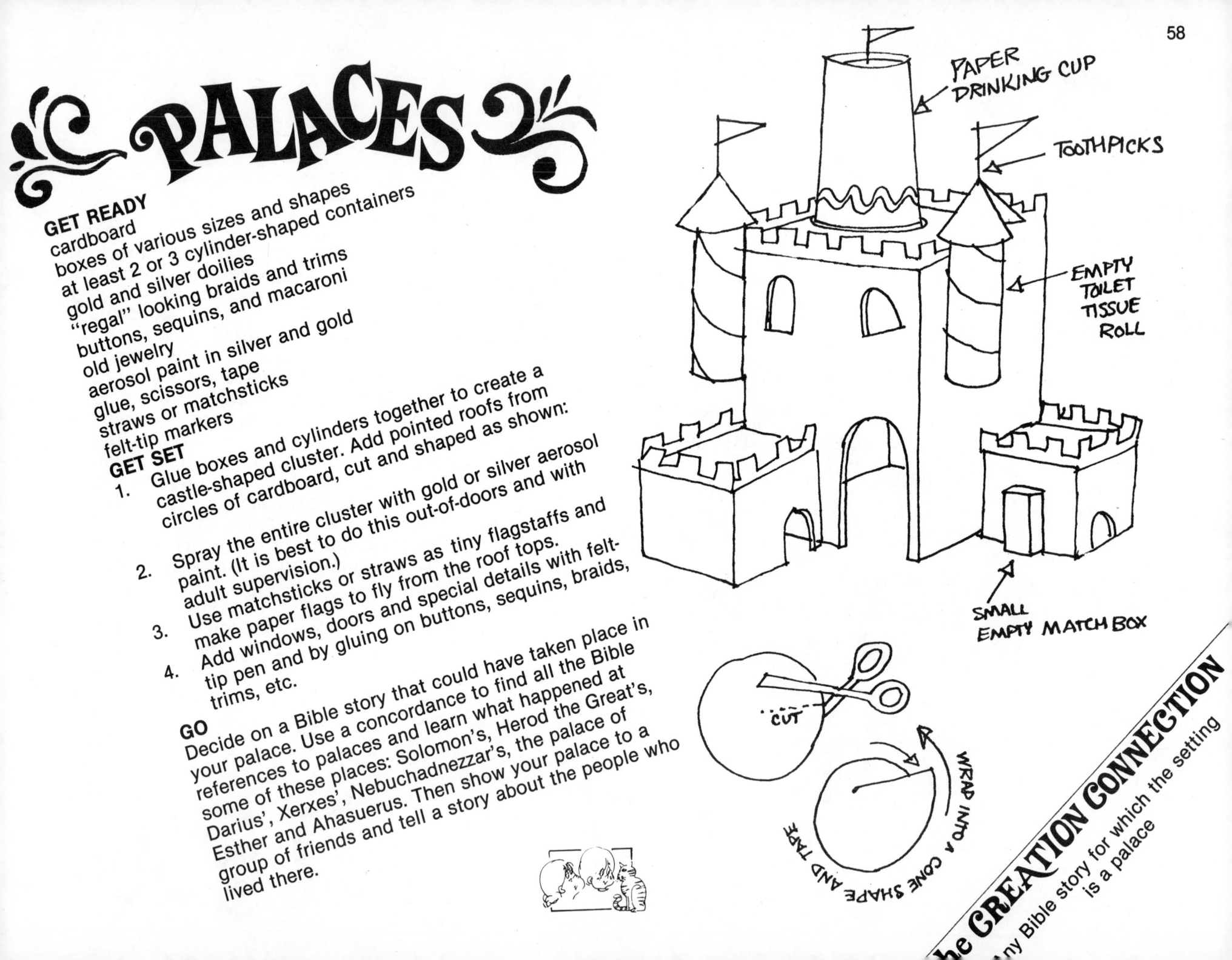

PAPER DRINKING CUP

TOOTHPICKS

EMPTY TOILET TISSUE ROLL

SMALL EMPTY MATCH BOX

CUT

WRAP INTO A CONE SHAPE AND TAPE

GET READY

cardboard
boxes of various sizes and shapes
at least 2 or 3 cylinder-shaped containers
gold and silver doilies
"regal" looking braids and trims
buttons, sequins, and macaroni
old jewelry
aerosol paint in silver and gold
glue, scissors, tape
straws or matchsticks
felt-tip markers

GET SET

1. Glue boxes and cylinders together to create a castle-shaped cluster. Add pointed roofs from circles of cardboard, cut and shaped as shown:

2. Spray the entire cluster with gold or silver aerosol paint. (It is best to do this out-of-doors and with adult supervision.)

3. Use matchsticks or straws as tiny flagstaffs and make paper flags to fly from the roof tops.

4. Add windows, doors and special details with felt-tip pen and by gluing on buttons, sequins, braids, trims, etc.

GO

Decide on a Bible story that could have taken place in your palace. Use a concordance to find all the Bible references to palaces and learn what happened at some of these places: Solomon's, Herod the Great's, Darius', Xerxes', Nebuchadnezzar's, the palace of Esther and Ahasuerus. Then show your palace to a group of friends and tell a story about the people who lived there.

The CREATION CONNECTION

Any Bible story for which the setting is a palace

GET READY

4 cups flour
2 cups water
1 cup salt
mixing bowl, spoon
rolling pin
waxed paper
strings

table knife or small
  cookie cutters
a drinking straw
oven
cookie sheet
tempera or acrylic
  paints and brushes
clear varnish

GET SET

1. Mix the ingredients together in a bowl to make dough.
2. Roll the dough out flat and use a knife or cookie cutters to cut whatever shapes you wish. DO NOT EAT THE DOUGH . . . YUK!!
3. Use a straw to poke a hole through each bead.
4. Place beads on wax paper and let them dry overnight.
5. Preheat oven to 300°.
6. Bake beads for one hour on ungreased cookie sheet.
7. Cool and decorate with paints.
8. Let paint dry thoroughly.
9. Cover each bead with a coat of clear varnish and dry.

GO

String the beads to make necklaces, belts, bracelets, shade pulls, mobiles, or decorations.

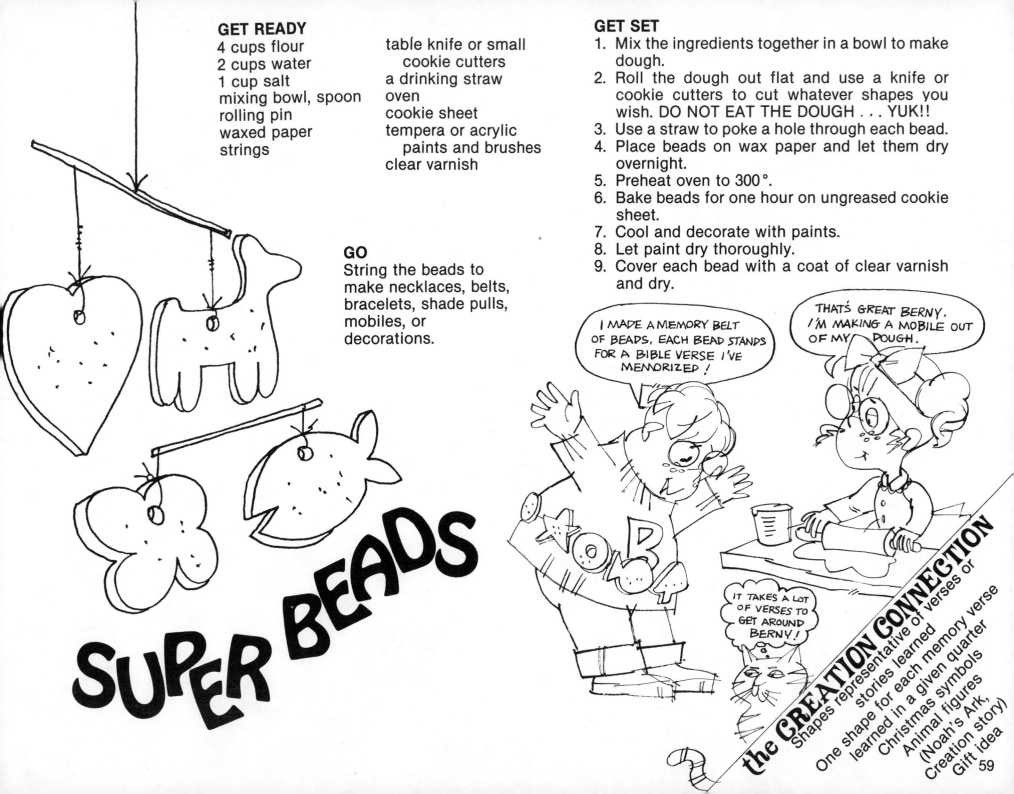

SUPER BEADS

I MADE A MEMORY BELT OF BEADS. EACH BEAD STANDS FOR A BIBLE VERSE I'VE MEMORIZED!

THAT'S GREAT BERNY. I'M MAKING A MOBILE OUT OF MY DOUGH.

IT TAKES A LOT OF VERSES TO GET AROUND BERNY!

the CREATION CONNECTION
Shapes representative of verses or stories learned
One shape for each memory verse learned in a given quarter
Christmas symbols
Animal figures
(Noah's Ark, Creation story)
Gift idea

SPIN-A-STORY

GET READY
old Sunday school papers or an old
  Bible storybook that can be cut up
a large, plain paper plate
a brass paper fastener
a collar stave (or substitute a
  diaper pin)
ruler, pencil, paste

GET SET
1. Cut from old Sunday school papers or a Bible story-book colored pictures that represent six different Bible stories.
2. Divide the paper plate into six equal sections.
3. Cut the six pictures to fit, one in each section of the plate, and paste them in place.
4. Make a spinner by using a sharp pointed object to make a hole in the center of a plastic collar stave. Attach it to the very center of the plate with a brass paper fastener. (OR use the fastener to attach a large diaper pin to the plate.)

GO
Invite a friend or a smaller child to spin-a-story by flicking the spinner. When the spinner stops, you must tell the story of the picture to which the spinner is pointing.

The CREATION CONNECTION
Six Bible stories of your choosing
Telling others about God

THE GREAT BRAIN

GET READY
a cardboard box, large
   enough to sit inside
crayons, felt-tip markers
scissors or knife
3 X 5 cards
pen or pencil

GET SET
1. Decorate the outside surface of the box to look like a giant computer.
2. Cut an IN slot on one side of the box and an OUT slot on the other side.
3. Make up a list of ten to twenty questions to which the answers are numbers.

Examples:
   How many sons did Noah have?
   How many books in the Old Testament?
   How many days was Jonah in the belly
      of the fish?
   How many loaves of bread did Jesus
      use to feed five thousand?
4. Write each question on a card.
5. Write the correct answer to each question on another card.
6. Place all the answer cards inside the computer.
7. Place all the question cards on top of the computer.

GO
Invite your friends to choose a question and feed it to the computer. You play the "Great Brain" by sitting inside the computer and giving OUT the answer.

NOTE:

It might be fun to place the computer's open side toward a wall and keep the "brain" a secret. Invite friends who don't know what's inside to try the computer. When the secret is revealed, take turns being the "brain."

the **CREATION CONNECTION**
Any set of Bible Questions and Answers

MAGIC PICTURES

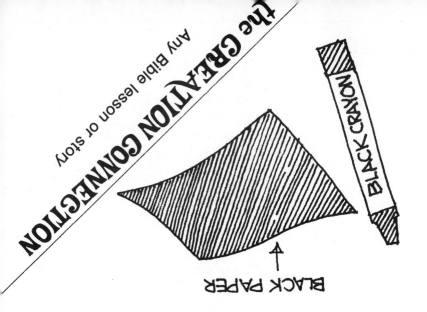

GET READY
black construction paper
pencil
black crayon
thin, white or yellow paint and
brush

GET SET
1. Think of a drawing you could make which illustrates something you learned recently in a Bible lesson. Don't tell anyone your idea!
2. Draw it lightly on black construction paper with your pencil. (Use the blackest side of your paper.)
3. Then trace over it with a black crayon, pressing VERY HARD.

GO
Give your black-on-black drawing to a friend and ask him to discover your secret idea by brushing a thin coat of white or yellow paint over the surface of your picture. When the picture appears, see if your friend can guess what your Bible lesson was about. If not, tell him!

The CREATION CONNECTION
Any Bible lesson or story

BLACK PAPER

BLACK CRAYON

GET READY
old magazines
scissors
paste
plain paper

GET SET
1. Choose a favorite Bible story. (See some suggestions on this page.) Find the story in the Scriptures and read it carefully. Make a mental note of important details.
2. Cut words, letters, and phrases from old magazines and use them to "rewrite" the story as it might appear in today's newspaper.
3. Write the title in headline style!

GO
Ask some friends to do stories too. Exchange and read each other's stories. Find a place to display the stories or make a scrapbook of them so that others may enjoy them too. (Perhaps you could submit them to your school paper or place the collection of stories in the church or school library.)

STORY SUGGESTIONS

THREE BOYS UNBURNABLE BY FIRE!
(Dan. 3:8-30)
FATHER TOLD TO KILL SON
(Gen. 22:1-19)
PLAGUES DRIVE EGYPT CRAZY
(Ex. 7:14-10:29)
BOY SLAYS GIANT (I Sam. 17:1-58)
MYSTERIOUS HAND APPEARS ON
WALL (Dan. 5:1-31)
MAN SURVIVES THREE DAYS INSIDE A
FISH! (Jonah 1:1-2:10)
BRAVE QUEEN SAVES HER PEOPLE
(Esther 2:5-8:17)
MAN RETURNS FROM THE DEAD!
(John 11:1-44)

WALLS OF JERICHO FALL

Surprise! That's how A Small group of Believers who responded to God's direction managed to Eliminate a BIG problem.

the CREATION CONNECTION
See suggested stories on this page

Lend a little LOVE ♥

GET READY

paper
scissors
crayons or felt-tip pens
pencil

GET SET

1. Use paper, crayons, and scissors to make some love coupons like the ones on this page.

2. Each day for a week, find at least one person who needs a special friend or a little extra love.

GO

Offer that person a coupon that gives him/her the privilege of using for a few days something special that belongs to you. Enjoy the good feeling of giving and sharing with others.

precious possessions
(like a bike, teddy bear, books, a special
blanket or pillow, sleeping bag, a ring,
etc..., OR your very own self as a baby-
sitter, companion, or friend)
a loving heart

COOKIE COUPON

THIS COUPON ENTITLES YOU TO HOMEMADE COOKIES MADE ESPECIALLY TO SHARE WITH A FRIEND! (ME!)

THIS COUPON ENTITLES YOU TO 3 HOURS OF FREE SERVICE FROM T.L.C. BABYSITTERS INC. REDEEMABLE AT YOUR REQUEST!

LAURA'S ♥ LENDING LIBRARY OFFERS YOU ANY 3 BOOKS FOR ONE WEEK EACH
TO:

ESPECIALLY FOR YOU:
A RIDE ON MY NEW BIKE
TO:

To with love
3 DAYS with MY TEDDY BEAR
THE WORLD'S GREATEST HUGGER

A SNOWMAN...

A REAL CUTE IDEA!

GET READY

snow	dried fruits
pine cone	cranberries
popcorn	sunflower seeds
peanut butter or suet	

GET SET

1. Roll snowballs to make a big snowman.
2. Use strong twigs (already fallen from trees) for ARMS.
3. Stuff a pine cone with suet or peanut butter and use as a nose.
4. Make prune EYES, a MOUTH of raisins or dates, and dried apricot BUTTONS.
5. Add a BELT of popcorn and cranberries, strung and twisted together.
6. Add a HAT with a band of popcorn or sunflower seeds tucked alongside a fabric band.
7. Set a large bucket of pan of water close to the snowman and check it several times a day to be sure it is not frozen solid.

GO

Enjoy watching birds and small animals being fed by the jolly snowman. Thank God for snow ... and birds ... and seeds and fruit and popcorn.

FOR THE BIRDS

the CREATION CONNECTION
Enjoying God's creation at work!

GET SET

1. Cut a hole in one side of the bottle to make a cockpit.
2. Cut propeller, wing, and tail shapes from the plastic lids or trays.
3. Make two slits beneath the cockpit, one on each side of the plane.
4. Push wing through the slits, also making cockpit seat.
5. Use same method to insert tail in back.
6. Use nail to poke a hole in the center of the propeller and in the nose of the plane.
7. Fasten propeller to plane by putting brass fastener through both holes and bending ends inside the nose of the plane.
8. Poke holes in the plane where you want to attach wheels.
9. Fasten wheels together by feeding pipe cleaners through holes and wheels and bending ends so wheels won't fall off.

MISSIONARY PILOT

CUT SLIT FOR TAIL.

SLIDE WINGS THROUGH SLITS IN SIDES OF BOTTLE.

PUNCH HOLE IN BOTTOM OF BOTTLE AND FASTEN WITH PAPER BRAD.

PIPE CLEANER THROUGH A LID HOLDS ON WHEEL.

CUT PROPELLER FROM PLASTIC LID.

GET READY

plastic detergent bottle with top
3 plastic bottle tops
2 pipe cleaners
large plastic lids (*i.e.,* cottage cheese containers)
 OR styrofoam meat trays)
scissors
1 nail
1 brass fastener

GO

Make several planes. Plan a landing field and a tower. Pretend you are a missionary pilot who can help people far from civilization by bringing missionaries, medical supplies, food, etc., to their villages.

GET READY

your Bible

a square (or nearly square) box with plain sides
  (You may paint the entire box with a light-colored,
  quick-drying enamel.)

paint and/or colored felt-tip pens

GET SET

1. Choose, from the list on this page, four miracles
    of Jesus that you would like to illustrate and tell
    about.
2. Look up the four references in your Bible and
    read the story of each miracle carefully. Decide
    what part of each miracle story you will illustrate
    and how.
3. Use the top surface of your box for a title.
4. Then use the four side surfaces to illustrate your
    miracle stories (one side for each story). Give
    each one an interesting title.
5. NOW, place the module on its top side. Create
    on the very bottom side an illustration of a
    modern-day miracle you might ask Jesus to
    perform if He were here on earth today.

GO

Prepare to share your first five surfaces with family
and friends. Share the bottom side of your miracle
module if you wish! Keep the finished module in your
room where it will remind you of the power of Jesus
Christ in people's lives. Do you think Jesus really
does perform miracles today?

MIRACLES

Wine for a wedding party — John 2:1-11
A man with four friends on a rooftop —
  Mark 2:1-12
Multiplying a boy's lunch — Mark 6:30-44
At the tomb of Lazarus — John 11:1-44
A blind beggar outside Jericho —
  Luke 18:35-43
A lame man — John 5:1-18
A Roman officer's servant — Luke 7:1-10
A young girl — Mark 5:21-24,35-43
A storm on the Sea of Galilee —
  Matt. 14:24-33

MIRACLE MODULE

the CREATION CONNECTION

All the "miracles" stories

SOLDIERS STRAIGHT & TALL

GET READY
cardboard tubes from toilet paper
red, black, and white construction paper
scissors
paste
felt-tip marker

GET SET
1. Cut colored paper to fit around the cardboard tubes.
2. Glue a narrow strip of white paper to the tube at about the place where the face should appear.
3. Glue a strip of black paper above the white to make a hat.
4. Glue a wider strip of red paper under the white strip to make clothing.
5. Use a marker to draw in face and any other features you wish.

GO
Make a whole army of soldiers. Stand them straight. Think about the qualities a good soldier must have. Make a list of words and phrases that tell about a good soldier.

EMPTY TOILET PAPER TUBE

BLACK PAPER

WHITE PAPER

RED PAPER

the CREATION CONNECTION
"Good soldiers" of Jesus Christ (2 Timothy 2:3-4)
Naaman, the Syrian captain
Roman soldiers
any story about soldiers, battles

LIVING MESSAGES

GET READY
soil
flower seeds (of small flowers)
sticks and strings
water
garden tools

GET SET
1. Choose a patch of very fine soil.
2. Write your message in the soil with a stick. (Try to make large, clear letters.)
   Ex. GOD IS LOVE   JOEY LOVES YOU
3. Shake the seeds of small flowers into the grooves you have traced in the soil.
4. Cover carefully with soil and keep the patch watered.
5. Use string and sticks to mark off the area, so you will know where it is until the flowers come up.

GO · · · GROW !
Watch your message grow in living color.
Tend it and weed it carefully so that it will bring joy to others.

LOOK! IT WORKED! IT WORKED! I PLANTED THE WORD OF GOD AND IT GREW!

WOW! THAT'S NEAT!

the CREATION CONNECTION
Any brief Bible verse, phrase, or message.

HERB OIL AND VINEGAR

In Bible times, people had to grow and make nearly all of their food. They used many herbs and spices to flavor and preserve their foods. Try this recipe for making an oil or vinegar dressing very much like the ones they made over a thousand years ago.

GET READY

4 or 5 sprigs of fresh tarragon, mint, or thyme
1 pt. of olive oil OR wine or cider vinegar
a tall jar or bottle with a tight lid or cork

GET SET

1. Hold each sprig of herbs in your hand. Do NOT remove the leaves, but rub them or roll them tightly between your fingers until you can smell the scent of the herb very strongly.
2. Place the sprigs in a tall bottle and add the oil OR vinegar.
3. Cover or cork tightly and shake.
4. Let it stand for four to six weeks before using so that the oil or vinegar will be flavorful.

GO

After six weeks, surprise your family by serving a salad sprinkled with your very own dressing OR tie a yarn ribbon and card on the bottle and give it as a gift to someone special.

IT'S REAL GOOD! (IT'S MY VERY OWN RECIPE!)

ALIZABETH'S OWN VINEGAR

The CREATION CONNECTION
Bible-time foods
Gift idea

SHADOW STORIES

GET READY
overhead projector
a variety of small objects which
project different sizes and
shapes
pencil and paper
colored acetate sheets (optional)

GET SET
1. Choose a Bible story that you think could be retold using just light, shadow, and color—no sound effects or narration allowed.
2. Use the light platform of an overhead projector as your "stage."
3. Choose a small object that has some representative shape for each character.

EXAMPLES:

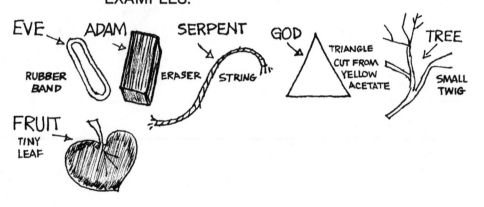

EVE — RUBBER BAND
ADAM — ERASER
SERPENT — STRING
GOD — TRIANGLE CUT FROM YELLOW ACETATE
TREE — SMALL TWIG
FRUIT — TINY LEAF

GO
Tell the story you have chosen by simply moving the shapes about on the light platform so that their shadows play out the character parts to dramatize the story. (It's just like doing a puppet show without words ... only the "puppets" are flat on the light platform instead of being held upright.)

Large sheets of colored acetate can change any part of the light platform or all of it to give the effect of different backgrounds or to create "day" and "night." Be creative! Try several stories. Present them as plays, mini-dramas, and light shows for your friends and family. Remember ... no SOUND!

the CREATION CONNECTION

Any story or biblical concept or truth that can be presented through this medium. Caution: Kids will be much better at this than adults.

THE WONDERFUL WORLD of COLOR!

WOW! THIS IS GREAT! EVERYTHING LOOKS GREEN OR RED OR BLUE!

WHO'S THAT FLOYD?...

BEATS ME! BUT THEY LOOK LIKE MOVIE STARS!

God loves color! Blue, purple, and scarlet are all mentioned more than fifty times each in the Bible. Aren't you glad God made color? (If He had not, our whole world would be shades of gray and black.) He did a good job, too—choosing exactly the right colors for the right things! Can you imagine skies being brown or red or green most of the time? He made everything just perfect and then He let us learn how to enjoy using His beautiful colors. This activity is a fun experiment with God's colors.

GET READY

tag or poster board
acetate or cellophane (red, yellow, and blue)
clear tape
scissors
paper fastener

GET SET

1. Use the pattern on this page to cut three pairs of eyeglasses from tag or poster board. Cut red acetate or cellophane to fit the lens area of one pair; cut yellow lenses for the second pair, and blue lenses for the third pair.

2. Tape each colored lens in place with clear tape on the backside of the glasses.

3. Now, poke a hole in the upper corner of all three pairs of glasses, and fasten the three pairs together with a paper fastener.

GO

Use your glasses separately and in different color combinations to look at the indoor and outdoor worlds around you. Think how exciting and marvelous color is and how brilliant and sensitive God is to have created something so amazingly beautiful and useful for us to enjoy. Thank Him. When you are tired of your glasses, send them to a child who is sick at home or in the hospital!

the CREATION CONNECTION

Wonder and praise at God's creation of color.

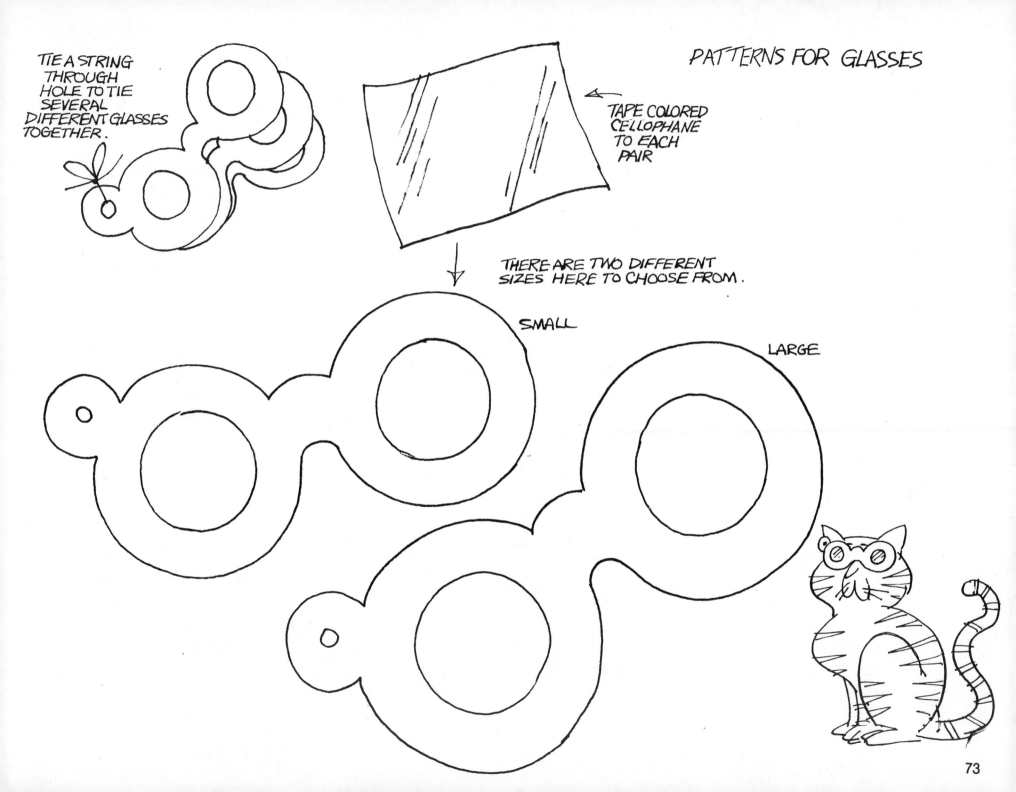

TIE A STRING THROUGH HOLE TO TIE SEVERAL DIFFERENT GLASSES TOGETHER.

TAPE COLORED CELLOPHANE TO EACH PAIR

THERE ARE TWO DIFFERENT SIZES HERE TO CHOOSE FROM.

SMALL

LARGE

WINTER WATER SCENE

GET READY

a heavy piece of cardboard
a small mirror (or piece of mirror)
sprigs of pine, greens, pine cones
play clay or plasticine
small objects appropriate to the scene or story
cotton balls and salt for snow
   (winter scenes only)

GET SET

1. Set your mirror in the center of a piece of card-board not much larger than the mirror.

2. Using the mirror as a lake, sea or pond, create surrounding scenery of trees and bushes by set-ting small sprigs, greens, and pine cones in play clay or plasticine. (If you are making a winter scene, dab edges of everything with glue and sprinkle with salt.)

3. Add cotton and salt to trees and edges of the water (winter scene only).

4. Place small appropriate objects on the water. (Dollhouse-size figures are appropriate.)

GO

Use your water or winter scene as a centerpiece for your dining table, coffee table, or desk.

the CREATION CONNECTION

Jesus calms the sea OR teaches from an
offshore boat
Peter walks on the water to meet Jesus
Noah's ark
Winter scenes
Christmas centerpieces

A "Magic" Bottle Message

It will take some time for the "magic" in this activity to happen, but it's worth it!

GET READY

a bearing fruit tree, just at the blossom time
a clear small-necked bottle
heavy paper or small card
permanent felt-tip pen
heavy tape

GET SET

1. Locate a fruit tree at blossom time—just when the fruit first begins to appear.
2. Use permanent felt-tip pen to write this message on a small card or slip of heavy paper:

   MADE IN _____
                  city, state

   by GOD, _____ .
                  season, year

3. Bend the paper just enough to slip it through the neck of the bottle.
4. Then slip the neck of the bottle over a tiny, healthy-looking piece of young fruit which is growing on the tree. Secure the bottle to the branch with heavy tape if necessary.
5. Check on your fruit each day . . . Enjoy watching it grow inside the bottle.
6. When the fruit is nearly grown, clip that branch as close to the bottle as possible.

GO

Display your "magic" bottle with its special message for your friends and family. (They will never to able to figure out how you got that big piece of fruit through the small neck of the bottle!)

THEN ALL YA NEED IS A STRAW WITH TEETH!

the CREATION CONNECTION

God, the Creator, the Source of growth

75

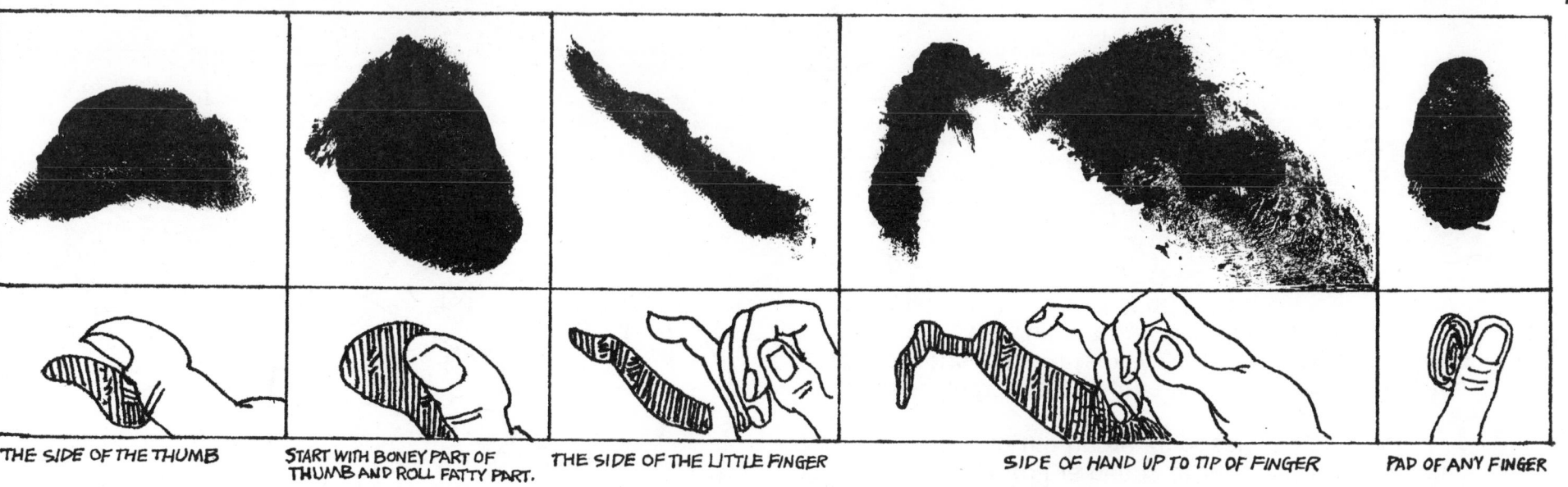

THE SIDE OF THE THUMB   START WITH BONEY PART OF THUMB AND ROLL FATTY PART.   THE SIDE OF THE LITTLE FINGER   SIDE OF HAND UP TO TIP OF FINGER   PAD OF ANY FINGER

THE WORLD'S "HANDIEST" PRINTING PRESS

SHEEP

GET READY
tempera paints

old food trays or plates • your hands • paper

GET SET

1. Create a picture of an object from one of your favorite Bible stories by using your hands and fingers as printing blocks.

2. Use an old meat tray or paper plate to hold each color of paint. Make the paint so that it is not runny and not too thick.

3. Dip your finger, thumb, side of your hand, knuckles or fists into the paint. (Each part of your hand will make a different kind of print.) Then use it as a printer to press on paper.

GO

Experiment on scrap paper first until you're sure the paint is the proper thickness and you have learned how to use the different parts of your hands to get different shapes. Then you can create all sorts of wonderful effects for your paintings!

DONKEY

SIDE OF LITTLE FINGER

SIDE OF WHOLE THUMB

SIDE OF LITTLE FINGER

SHEPHERD

GRAPES

FLOWER

the CREATION CONNECTION

Any Bible story

PAPER STARS

SO SIMPLE TO MAKE!

GET READY
heavy paper (any colors)
pencil and eraser
scissors
thread or yarn

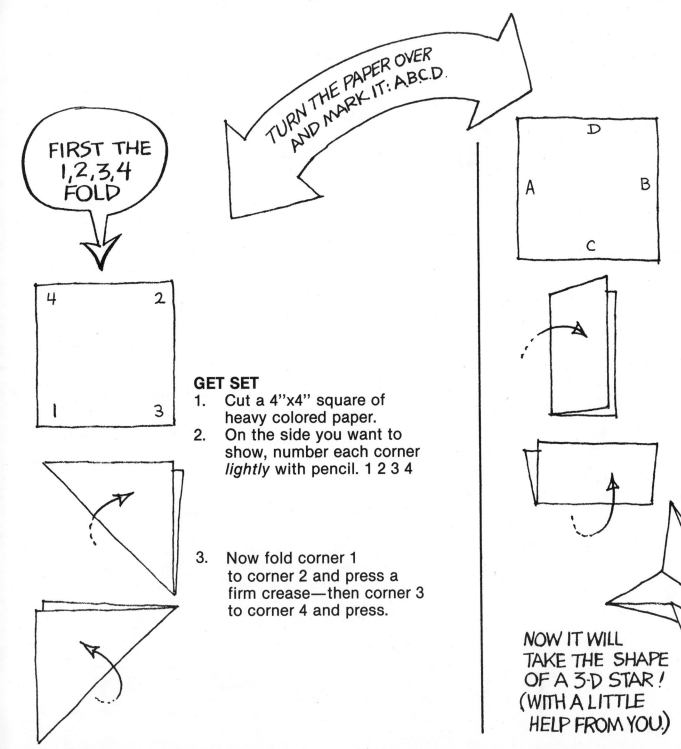

FIRST THE 1,2,3,4 FOLD

TURN THE PAPER OVER AND MARK IT: A,B,C,D.

...THEN THE A,B,C,D FOLD

GET SET
1. Cut a 4"x4" square of heavy colored paper.
2. On the side you want to show, number each corner *lightly* with pencil. 1 2 3 4
3. Now fold corner 1 to corner 2 and press a firm crease—then corner 3 to corner 4 and press.

4. **Turn the paper over** and *lightly* write the letters A B C D in the places shown.
5. Now fold side A to meet side B. Press hard along the fold to make a firm crease. Then fold side C to side D and press a firm crease.
6. Open the star and erase the numbers and letters.

GO
Pinch the corners of the star gently together and you will get a lovely, four-cornered, three-dimensional star. You can make many stars of different sizes by beginning with different size squares.

NOW IT WILL TAKE THE SHAPE OF A 3-D STAR! (WITH A LITTLE HELP FROM YOU.)

the **CREATION CONNECTION**

Christmas Creation story

ANIMAL MENAGERIE

(See how many of these animals you can make!)

GET READY

scissors
tape
felt-tip markers
empty match box
spools or big
  macaroni
green paint or
  marker
drinking straws
empty eggshell

cardboard scraps
string
egg carton
cotton balls
paper cups
pencil
paper
play clay

GET SET

Follow the directions to make each animal.

GO

Open your own zoo. Play Noah's Ark. (Make two of every animal. Use one of the people patterns in this book to make Noah and his family.) Think of a Bible story to go with each animal. Tell them to a friend.

WOW! WE CAN MAKE OUR OWN ZOO!

A FAT PIG

1. Tape two paper cups together for body.
2. With a nail, poke holes into body where legs should go.
3. Cut drinking straws short and insert for legs.
4. Make a curly tail by wrapping a long thin piece of paper tightly around a pencil. Then tape it to the pig's body.
5. Add floppy paper ears.
6. Paint pink or black and white spots and draw in face with marker.
7. Glue on an empty thread spool for a nose.

MILK BOX RABBIT

1. Cut two ears out of colored construction paper and glue on lid flap.
2. Cover box with white paper.
3. Draw face on one side.
4. Attach cotton ball on backside for tail.

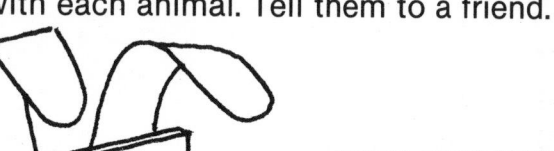

WHATS A MENAGERIE?

SAYS HERE IT'S A COLLECTION OF ANIMALS!

HUMAN TALK

GLAD THEY DIDN'T MAKE ANY CATS!

HEY LOOK, MARY KAY, I JUST MADE A CAT OUT OF A KITTY LITTER BOX!

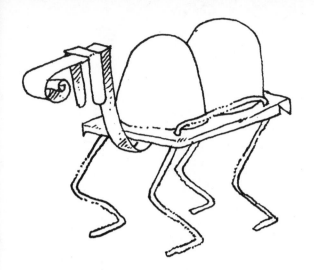

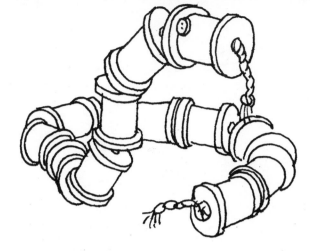

CARTON CAMEL

1. Cut two sections from an egg carton.
2. Paint brownish-tan.
3. Cut and glue on cardboard legs and head.
4. Add a string with a knot for a tail.

WIGGLY SNAKES

1. Thread spools or large macaroni on a string.
2. Tie big knots at each end and leave a short length of string for a tongue.
3. Paint each part of the snake with a different stripe or design.

SH ... SH ... SHEEP

1. Use an empty match box or any small box for a body.
2. Attach straws or used wooden matches for legs as shown.
3. Use a piece of clothesline rope with a knot for his nose tied at one end. Glue on yarn ears and a ball of cotton for his head. Glue rope to side of match box.

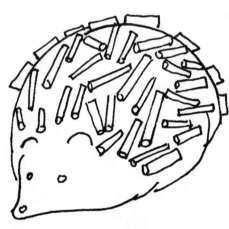

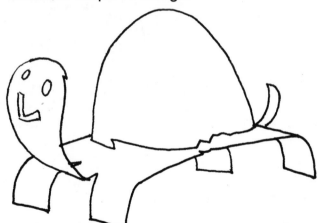

HARMLESS HEDGEHOG

1. Shape the hedgehog's body of play clay or dough.
2. Make his nose pointed and give him beady little eyes.
3. Cut straws into short length and press into body.

THE TORTOISE

1. Cut tortoise shape from cardboard.
2. Bend legs down and head up.
3. Paint him green and draw on eyes, mouth, and toes.
4. Crush empty eggshell into medium-size pieces and glue to tortoise's back.
5. Paint with a second coat of green.

the CREATION CONNECTION

Stories in which these animals appear (Nativity, Garden of Eden, Brass Serpent, etc.)

81

The Happy Helper

GET READY

pail, basket, or box
sponge or squeegee
paper towels or newspapers
dust cloth
spray window cleaner
pad and pencil
one piece of white construction
  paper
felt-tip marker
a special snack treat
gift card

GET SET

1. Assemble all tools in the pail, box or basket.
2. Use the construction paper to make an armband that says, "Hi, I'm your HAPPY HELPER" or something similar.
3. Make a gift card to stick in the top of your work pail.
4. Add a special fruit or cookie-type snack treat to share with the person you are helping.

GO

Give yourself as a present to someone who would be especially happy for your help. Offer to clean mirrors, windows, and glass doors, sinks and tubs; dust furniture, baseboards. Use your pad and pencil to take orders for other jobs that need to be done. Work hard . . . and SMILE!

The **CREATION CONNECTION**

Mother's or Father's Day gift
Gift to elderly person
who needs help
Giving and well-doing
others (Galatians 6:9)

YOUR SMILE ...('IT'S THE MOST IMPORTANT PART!)

HAPPY HELPER ..." AT WORK

SPECIAL CARD 7   LABEL FOR BOX OR CAN 5

ARM BAND 7

HAPPY HELPER ON THE JOB!

WRITE THE WORD "ME!" ON THE INSIDE OF THE CARD AFTER YOU HAVE FOLDED IT ALONG DOTTED LINE 7 SIGN YOUR NAME TOO!

ON THIS SPECIAL DAY... I'M GIVING YOU SOMETHING VERY SPECIAL...

How Does Your Garden Grow?

GET READY
an adult helper
1/4 cup salt
1/4 cup water
1/4 cup bluing
1 tablespoon ammonia
a mixing bowl and spoon
4 pieces of charcoal
  (break apart smooth brickettes to
  expose rough edges)
food coloring
glass pie plate or shallow dish

GET SET
1. Mix salt, water, bluing, and ammonia in a bowl.
2. Place charcoal with rough edges UP in the pie plate.
3. Pour the mixture over the charcoal pieces and sprinkle food coloring on the charcoal.
4. Set the dish in a warm place.

GO
DON'T LOOK for about forty-five minutes — then surprise yourself! Notice that little crystals have begun to form. The longer the mixture sits, the better it grows. Add a teaspoon of ammonia each week to keep your garden in "bloom." Think about who makes things like crystals grow. If you know the song, "God Is The First Cause," sing it while you watch your garden grow.

UM GLAD THAT'S NOT MY WATER DISH!

the CREATION CONNECTION
God is the source of all growing things.

GET READY

wooden spoons
acrylic paints OR permanent
felt-tip pens
pencil and paper
fabric trims, yarn, ribbons,
tiny buttons, beads, etc.
glue
small picture hanger
(optional)

GET SET

1. Choose a favorite Bible hero or heroine. (The list on this page may help you think of a very special one!)
2. Use a wooden cooking spoon to represent the face and body of this person.
3. Use your pencil to carefully sketch the person's face on the spoon. Then trace over your lines with paint or pen.
4. Add yarn for hair and beard, tiny buttons or beads for eyes, etc.
5. Add bows or beads, collars, etc. at the "neck."

GO

Write a short description of your hero or heroine as if the person were saying it. ("Hello! My name is Joshua ... I am a very adventuresome fellow ... etc.") Memorize your description. Then introduce "yourself" to everyone you meet.

Optional idea: Attach a small picture hanger to the back of your spoon person so that you can hang it on the wall in your room.

Solomon	Daniel	Isaac
David	Jeremiah	Paul
Nehemiah	Elijah	Lydia
Gideon	Jonah	Ruth
Joshua	John	Hannah
Abraham	Stephen	Esther
Joseph	Philip	Mary
Moses	Barnabas	Mary and Martha
Noah	Jacob	Dorcas

the CREATION CONNECTION

Also a great gift idea for Mother's Day (to hang in kitchen ... or an entire family of spoon people might stand upright in a jar ...) Bible heroes and heroines

85

TOOTHPASTE PICTURES

Zippo Tooth Paste

the CREATION CONNECTION
Sharing God's message of God's creation with others
Any Bible story
Creatures of God's creation

GET READY
several colors of toothpaste
(it comes in white, striped, red, and striped yellow, blue, green, deep yellow construction paper)

Use construction paper

GET SET
1. yellow pencil to draw. VERY LIGHTLY on an idea or object from a simple picture, a favorite Bible story OR you might choose a favorite Bible story creation such as a bird, butterfly, tiger, or sunflower.

2. Retrace your light pencil lines with one or more colors of toothpaste. Squeeze the tubes lightly to create a smooth, thin line squeeze harder and trace more slowly. Let the toothpaste dry.

3. **GO** Take your Bible picture with you on your next visit to your dentist and tell him or her the story of your picture!

WHY?... CAUSE IP GET SQUEEZED IN THE MIDDLE! I WOULD LIKE TO BE A TOOTHPASTE TUBE!

98

GET READY

2 1-quart milk cartons
clear plastic food wrap
2 large rubber bands
tape, scissors, pencil
a jar lid about 2½" across
an adult with a sharp knife

GET SET

1. Use a pencil and the jar lid to trace a perfect circle on the bottom of each milk carton.
2. VERY CAREFULLY, cut out the circle. Take care not to cut crookedly or tear the carton. The edges must be very smooth. When you finish cutting, smooth the edges with your thumb and finger.
3. Tear a large piece of plastic wrap and stretch it over the bottom of each carton. Hold it in place with a rubber band. Trim off the extra wrap, leaving about a half-inch below the rubber band. Use tape to keep it stretched tightly over each hole as a lens. Tape one side, then the opposite side. (Always tape alternate sides to keep the wrap taut.)
4. When each lens is tight and secure, use one long piece of tape to wrap around the entire edge of the lens to be sure no water can seep in. Now carefully remove the rubber bands.
5. Set the two cartons side by side on a table with lenses down flat on the table. Carefully slide a large rubber band down over both cartons to keep them together. Use another band to hold them together near the top.

GO

If you have an aquarium, test your binoculars there. Then find a pond or stream or lake where you can watch underwater life by putting the lenses just below the surface of the water.

Watch God's Underwater World

① CUT HOLE IN BOTTOM OF CARTON

② TAPE PLASTIC WRAP ON

③ SEAL PLASTIC WRAP

the CREATION CONNECTION
Observing God's creation in action

87

Mom & Dad Awards

GET READY
old magazines
flat, 3-dimensional objects that are
  appropriate to the subject
white glue
picture frame
cardboard or heavy construction paper
scissors

GET SET
1. Purchase a large picture frame OR find a used one.
2. Cut a piece of heavy cardboard or construction paper the size to fit the frame.
3. Cut from magazine words and pictures that remind you of the qualities, characteristics and special likes of your Mom or Dad. (Include hobbies, favorite foods, important dates, sports, prize possessions, etc.)
4. Collect additional items around the house that are typical of them—such as a flower, a shopping list, a toothpick, a recipe, a telephone number, business card, etc.

GO
Use your collection of pictures, words, and items to make a collage that is a special tribute to your Mom or Dad or both.

the CREATION CONNECTION
Mother's Day or Father's Day Gift Idea
"Honor your father and mother . . ."
(Exod. 20:12 LB)

SPICE IS NICE

In the Bible, spices are often mentioned. They were used to make ointments, perfumes, anointing oils, and were often offered as expensive gifts. This activity is an opportunity to make a gift of spices.

GET READY

whole cloves, cinnamon stick, nutmeg,
   and other whole spices
small, brightly-colored fabric scraps
3 yards heavy yarn
safety pins
yarn or ribbon scraps
pinking shears

GET SET

1. Cut three one-yard lengths of heavy yarn.
2. Hold the three pieces together and fold in the center to make a loop at one end and six strands at the other. Tie near the top with a yarn or ribbon scrap to secure the loop.
3. Now braid the strands, using two strands for each section of the braid. Tie the braid at the bottom with another yarn or ribbon scrap.
4. Cut three or four six-inch circles or squares of fabric from bright-colored fabric scraps.
5. Place a handful of spices in the center of each piece and tie with a ribbon or yarn bow.
6. Attach these pretty, spicy packages to your yarn "pigtail" at even intervals with a safety pin.

GO

Hang your spice rope in a place where you can enjoy its bright colors and sweet smell or give it to someone who especially needs a little bit of love.

the CREATION CONNECTION
Any Bible reference that mentions spices as gifts of value

AND GOD SAID, "LET THERE BE"...

GET READY

construction paper:
  white, green, brown, dark blue, light blue,
  purple, and yellow
felt-tip pen
scissors
patterns
stapler or yarn

GET SET

1. Read Psalm 104 aloud to yourself with exaggerated expression. (Use the Living Bible paraphrase if you have a copy.)
2. Trace and cut from construction paper a piece the exact size and color indicated by each pattern on these pages.
3. Do NOT copy the number and color name of each piece, But DO copy carefully the Scripture verse you see on each piece.
4. Fold piece #1 so that the piece opens like a book with the cut-out circle and verse on the front "cover."
5. Now lay piece #8 inside, matching its bottom edge with the bottom edge of the cover.
6. On TOP of pieces #8, lay piece #7, then #6, then #5 ... and so on, in order, with the remaining pattern pieces, until all eight pieces are in place. Be sure to keep bottom edges even. Then you will be able to see an entire "creation" picture through the open circle (frame) on the front cover.
7. Fasten your pages in place with staples or yarn.

GO

Read the book aloud to yourself and rejoice in God's wonderful creation. Read it aloud to someone else. Sing the Doxology or any other praise song you especially like. Share Psalm 104 and your booklet with your family and friends.

PRAISE GOD FOREVER HOW HE MUST REJOICE IN ALL HIS WORK!
PSALM 104:31

the CREATION CONNECTION

The Creation Story
Worship
Psalm 104

(#1 – WHITE)

**Trace the lines
on this page.
Cut on all the solid
lines. Fold on the
broken line. Use the
patterns to make
pages of these
shapes on colored
paper.**

FOLD▷

Praise God forever!
How he must rejoice in
all his work!
(Ps. 104:31 LB)

(#8 – LIGHT BLUE)

The heavens are yours,
the world, everything —
for you created them all.
(Ps. 89:11 LB)

(#4 – DARK BLUE)

(#3 – BROWN)

(#2 – LIGHT GREEN)

Then God said, "Let the
waters beneath the sky
be gathered into oceans ..."
(Gen. 1:9 LB)

The earth is full of the
goodness of the Lord.
(Ps. 33:5)

He lets me rest
in the meadow grass ...
(Ps. 23:2 LB)

Trace the lines on this page.
Cut on all the solid lines.
Use the patterns to make these shapes on colored paper.

ALL THESE LITTLE PAGES GO INTO THE COVER AND MAKE A PICTURE IN THE OVAL HOLE!

(#7-YELLOW)

And God made two great lights; the greater light to rule the day, and the lesser light to rule the night.
(Gen. 1:16)

(#5 - DARK GREEN)

... For the tree of the field is man's life ...
(Deut. 20:19)

I WROTE A STORY ONCE FOR KITTY CAT DIGEST.
IT WAS ALL ABOUT A LONELY, WAYWARD COCKERPOO!

(#6 - PURPLE)

You spoke, and at the sound of your shout ... mountains rose ...
(Ps. 104:7 LB)

GET READY
Colored chalk
paint smocks (in this
case, chalk smocks)
a sidewalk or blacktop
area
a happy feeling

GET SET
1. Greet a new spring or summer season by celebrating those first beautiful days with your very own "sidewalk art show" ... ON the sidewalk! Ask your friends to join you during a Sunday school class session. Do the entire sidewalk in front of the church or a section of the church parking lot with chalk pictures about the season's growth and life.

2. Then invite the entire congregation to visit the art show after church and celebrate the arrival of the new season with you. Ask someone to help you lead the congregation in a hymn of praise. Everyone might join hands as they sing together. (P.S. The first good rain or the janitor will clean the sidewalk!)

GO

CELEBRATE SPRING (OR SUMMER)

BERNY

REGIE

TOOTER

ALIZABETH

the **CREATION CONNECTION**

Celebration of a new season

93

The Honor of Your Presence!

GET READY
black ink pen or calligraphy set
plain heavy white paper
an etiquette book (optional)

GET SET
1. Surprise your friends by sending them an "engraved" invitation to a shocking historic event! (Choose one of these or pick your own.)
   BELSHAZZAR'S FEAST (featuring the hand-writing on the wall)—Daniel 5
   THE FALL OF MAN (featuring a crafty serpent—Genesis
   THE FALL OF JERICHO (featuring trumpets and shouting)—Joshua 6
   A WEDDING AT CANA (featuring a special guest)—John 2
   THE PARTING OF THE RED SEA (featuring the instant construction of a new highway)—Exodus 14
2. Check a book of etiquette such as Amy Vanderbilt's volume to see models for writing formal invitations.

GO
In your own stylized calligraphy, write a formal invitation to one of the shocking events in biblical history. Then prepare a pantomime, drama, or reading relating to the event to be presented upon the arrival of your invited guests.

King Belshazzar of Babylon requests the honor of your presence at a great feast with his officers, princes & wives... and a strange mystery guest.

Drinks at 8 o'clock... served from the gold & silver cups taken from the Temple at Jerusalem.

R.S.V.P.

Satan & 70 honor you distinguished guests at a party in Eden IS expertise in temptation...

Joshua and his entire army request the honor of your presence

You are cordially invited to an overnite chariot chase in celebration of the opening (and closing) of a new highway between Egypt & the Shur desert.

Since the highway will be open for such a short time, please be prompt...

the CREATION CONNECTION
Any outstanding, shocking event in biblical history

Make a MONSTER

GET READY
Bible (Job 41)
Art materials you choose

GET SET

1. Read Job 41, in which Job talks to God about the biggest and scariest sea monster ever. You will see a detailed description of this monster called a leviathan. Look up the word *leviathan* in your dictionary.

2. From the description in Job 41, create with materials you choose, a model of this enormous leviathan. You may draw, paint, sculpt, use paper, clay, or whatever art medium you think will best illustrate the monster.

GO
Share your grisly monster with friends and tell them Job's story. Why is the monster story in the book of Job? What effect did the idea of meeting this monster have on Job?

THERE'S A BUNCH OF LITTLE MONSTERS MAKING LITTLE MONSTERS!

the CREATION CONNECTION

Job 41
God's great power and sovereignty

Rules to Live By

GET READY

a flat, styrofoam block
(1"-1½" thick, at least 6"x8")
knife
white paper
typewriter or black pen
glue
Bible

GET SET

1. Cut a flat styrofoam block to represent the shape of ancient stone tablets.
2. Read the Ten Commandments from Exodus 20:1-17 in your Bible and think about what each one means. These are the rules that God has given to people to live by. They are not just for grownups. They are for boys and girls too.
3. Copy them from your Bible, but as you write them, try to paraphrase them in words that will be simple and have meaning for you.
4. Type or write in black ink your Ten Commandments in two lists of five to fit the "tablets" you have made. Cut and paste them in place on the tablets.

GO

Keep them where they can be a reminder to you and your family that God wants you to observe these rules carefully as you live each day.

I. "I AM THE LORD... YOU SHALL HAVE NO OTHER GODS BEFORE ME."

II. "YOU SHALL NOT MAKE ANY IDOLS TO WORSHIP."

III. "YOU SHALL NOT TAKE THE NAME OF THE LORD YOUR GOD IN VAIN."

IV. "REMEMBER THE SABBATH DAY TO KEEP IT HOLY."

V. "HONOR YOUR FATHER AND YOUR MOTHER."

VI. "YOU SHALL NOT COMMIT MURDER."

VII. "YOU SHALL NOT COMMIT ADULTERY."

VIII. "YOU SHALL NOT STEAL."

VIIII. "YOU SHALL NOT GIVE A FALSE TESTIMONY."

X. "YOU SHALL NOT COVET."

STYROFOAM BLOCK

the CREATION CONNECTION
Ten Commandments (Exodus 20:1-17)

COME-ALIVE MURAL

GET READY
a favorite Bible story
mural-size paper
pencil, crayons or
  paint
scissors
tape

GET SET
1. Choose a favorite Bible story.
2. Invite your friends to listen as you read the story aloud.
3. Work together to plan a mural about your story. Plan it so that it can have several "moving" parts. These can be created by cutting holes or slits in the finished mural through which you can insert real arms, legs, hands, faces, etc.
4. Tape the finished mural securely between two chairs or ladders or someplace where there is hidden space behind the mural for the live actors.

GO
Invite your families to come to see your live mural. Take your places behind the mural and tell the story by using the mural with its moving parts.

the CREATION CONNECTION

Any Bible story

STORYBOOK PEOPLE

GET READY
L'Eggs stocking eggs OR styrofoam cups
spring-type clothespins
permanent felt-tip pens

GET SET
1. Use halves of a L'Eggs stocking egg OR styrofoam cups as bodies for your story people.
2. Add faces with permanent felt-tip pens.
3. Clip three clothespins onto the edge of each egg half or cup to make legs for your story people.

GO
Use your story people as the characters or actors for a favorite Bible story or play you would like to do for your friends.

Note: Five-ounce and three-ounce paper cups may be used (with jumbo paper clips for legs) to represent smaller people . . . like children . . .

VERY STRANGE!

the CREATION CONNECTION
Any Bible story

Walk Through the Bible — A PICTURE EXHIBITION!

GET READY

you and your artistic friends —
  all ages
all sorts of art media, materials
a place that can be used as an
  exhibit hall
resource books such as:
> *The Children's Bible,* Golden Press,
>   New York
> *The Young Readers' Bible, RSV,*
>   A. J. Holman Co., Philadelphia,
>   Pennsylvania
> *The Book of Life,* The Zondervan
>   Corp., Grand Rapids, Michigan

GET SET

1. Invite friends and acquaintances of all ages who
    are interested in art to submit a drawing, painting,
    sculpture, mobile, collage, etc. for an exhibit of
    art that is representative of a Bible story or
    concept.

2. Each entry should be labeled with the artist's
    name and a title that relates to the Bible story
    with which it is associated.

3. Set a deadline for entries and appoint a place to
    which all entries should be delivered.

4. Ask a committee of kids and grownups to help
    you arrange the exhibit in the order that the
    events these entries represent occurred in the
    Bible. (Use the resource books as your guides.)
    Then number each entry and create a program
    guide for visitors to the exhibit.

GO

Invite the entire community to "walk through the
Bible" by visiting your exhibit.

BY WART AND GOD MADE CATS!

BY BERNIE
PLAGUES IN EGYPT

BY BERNICE
MOSES & THE RED SEA

DID THIS ONE SAMUEL. ISN'T IT PRECIOUS?

the CREATION CONNECTION
Biblical stories and concepts
expressed through various
art media

PAPER STRIP RABBIT TREATS

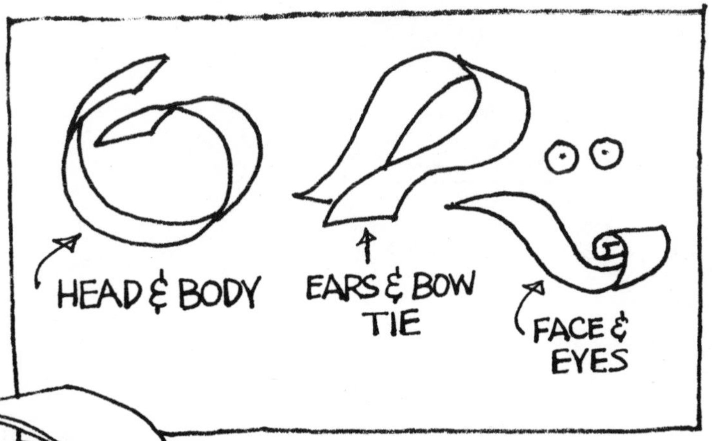

HEAD & BODY   EARS & BOW TIE   FACE & EYES

GET READY
Strips of paper
  (any colors)
glue
cotton balls
scissors
nut cup
nuts, candies, or raisins

GET SET
1. Use paper strips, scissors, and glue to create a rabbit similar to the ones on this page.
2. Add a cotton-ball tail and a brightly-colored bow tie.
3. Anchor by placing tiny nut cup filled with nuts, raisins, or candies inside largest circle. Fasten to circle with tape or glue.

GO
Multiply your efforts and make a whole family of rabbits OR use your own ingenuity to create other paper-strip animals in the same way.

the CREATION CONNECTION

Creation
Noah's ark
Spring/Easter

PAINT ME....

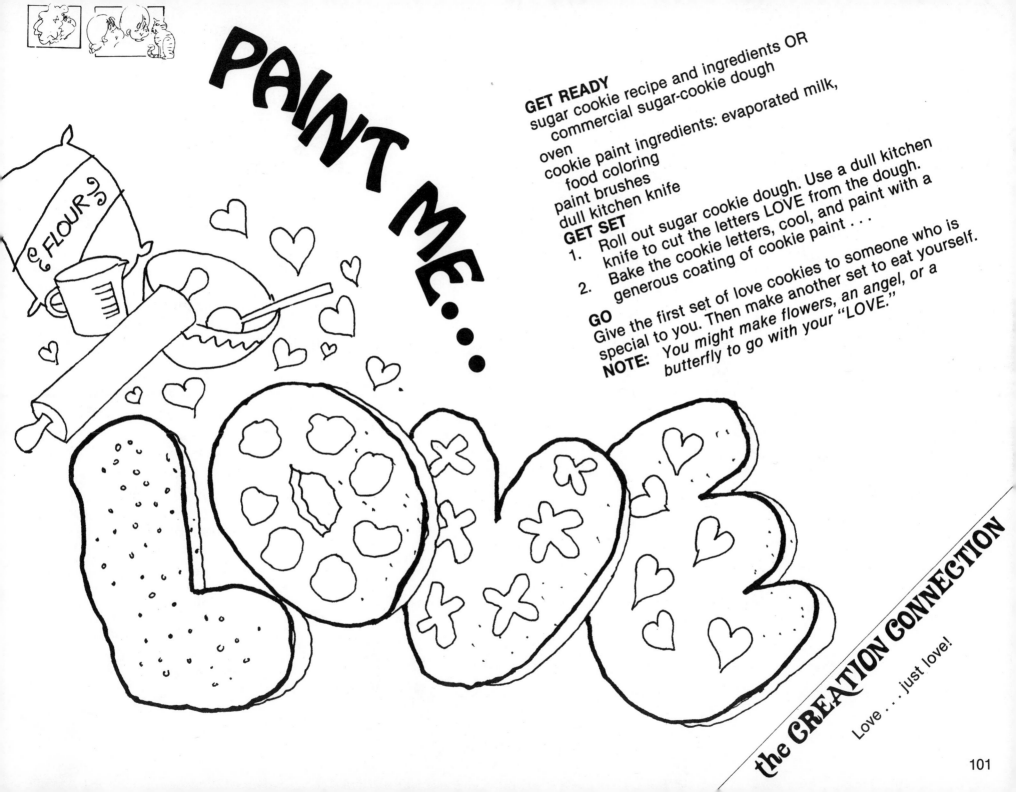

GET READY
sugar cookie recipe and ingredients OR
   commercial sugar-cookie dough
oven
cookie paint ingredients: evaporated milk,
   food coloring
paint brushes
dull kitchen knife

GET SET
1. Roll out sugar cookie dough. Use a dull kitchen knife to cut the letters LOVE from the dough.
2. Bake the cookie letters, cool, and paint with a generous coating of cookie paint . . .

GO
Give the first set of love cookies to someone who is special to you. Then make another set to eat yourself.

NOTE: You might make flowers, an angel, or a butterfly to go with your "LOVE."

the CREATION CONNECTION

Love . . . just love!

A Simple Star

GET READY

styrofoam meat tray or piece of
 cardboard
yellow construction paper
yellow yarn or ribbon
a nail
scissors
glue

GET SET

1. Place a piece of yellow construc-
    tion paper under this page and
    trace the size star that best fits on
    your styrofoam tray or cardboard.
    Press hard so that the tracing will
    make an impression on the yellow
    paper.
2. Cut out the star, put a dot of glue
    on the center back, and press it in
    place on the tray or cardboard.
3. Use a nail to poke holes at the
    points and angles of the star
    (through both the yellow paper AND the
    backing). Then "sew" the star to the
    background with yellow yarn or ribbon.
4. Poke a hole at the top of the background
    board and string a loop of yarn or ribbon
    through to use as a hanger.

GO

Hang your star on a Christmas tree or in your
room where it can remind you of the star that
led the Wise Men to Jesus.

DID SOMEONE SAY SOMETHING ABOUT A MEAT TRAY?

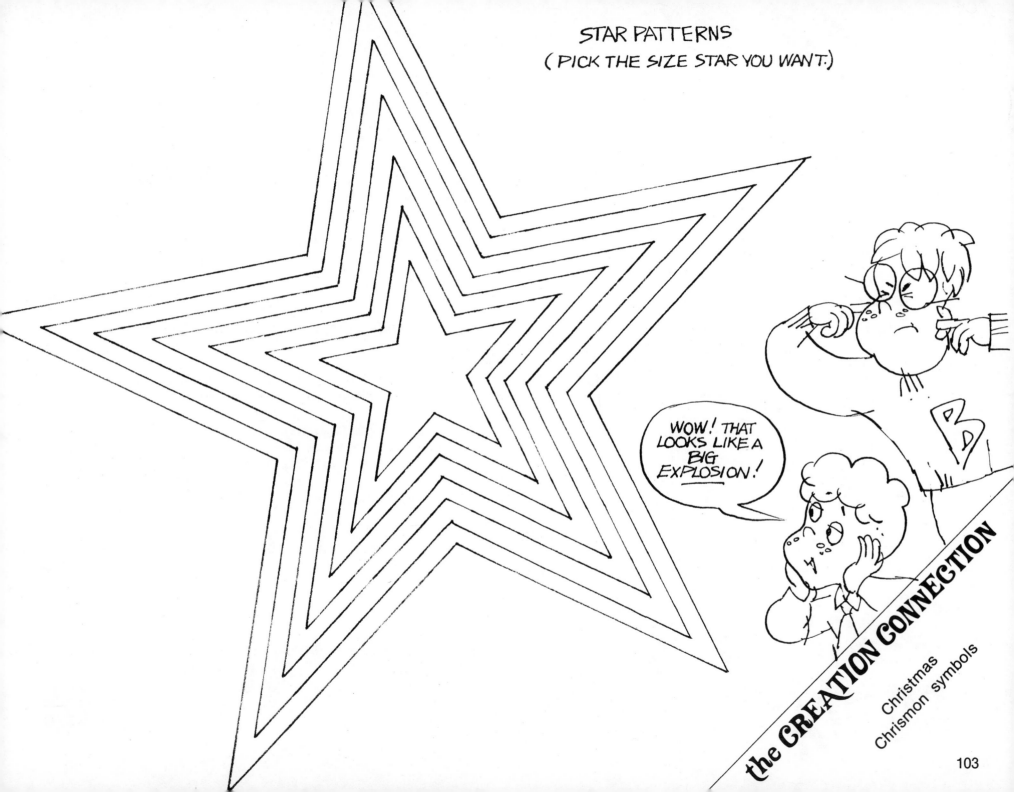

GET READY

white construction paper
gold foil wrapping paper (OR substitute
   yellow construction paper)
several bright colors of construction paper
scissors
paste
pen or pencil
Bible

GET SET

1. Use the pattern on this page to make five kings
(OR you may choose just one king and get four
friends to do the others, then share.)
2. Make your king(s) so that their royal robes open
to reveal a secret writing surface.
3. Then read the stories of the five unusual kings.
Across each king's outspread robe, write his story
in your own words. In just a few brief sentences,
tell what was unusual about him.
4. Then wrap each king's robe tightly around him,
concealing his story, until you are ready to read it
again.

GO

Stand your kings in stately order on a table where
other people will become curious to read the inside
stories and share what you have learned.

FIVE UNUSUAL KINGS

1. The king with the big bed (KING OG) Deut. 3:11
2. The cruel king (KING MANASSEH) 2 Kings 21:1-18,
2 Chron. 33:10-20
3. The king who pretended to be crazy (KING DAVID)
1 Sam. 21:10-15
4. The king who cut off thumbs and toes (KING
ADONI-BEZEK) Judg. 1:1-7
5. The king who turned into an animal (KING
NEBUCHADNEZZAR (Dan. 4:28-37)

ALL KINDS OF KINGS

KING OG
ONCE THERE WAS A KING IN THE LAND OF BASHAN WHO HAD AN IRON BED THAT WAS MORE THAN 13 FEET LONG AND 6 FEET WIDE!

AMAZING!

the CREATION CONNECTION
Five kings of the Old Testament

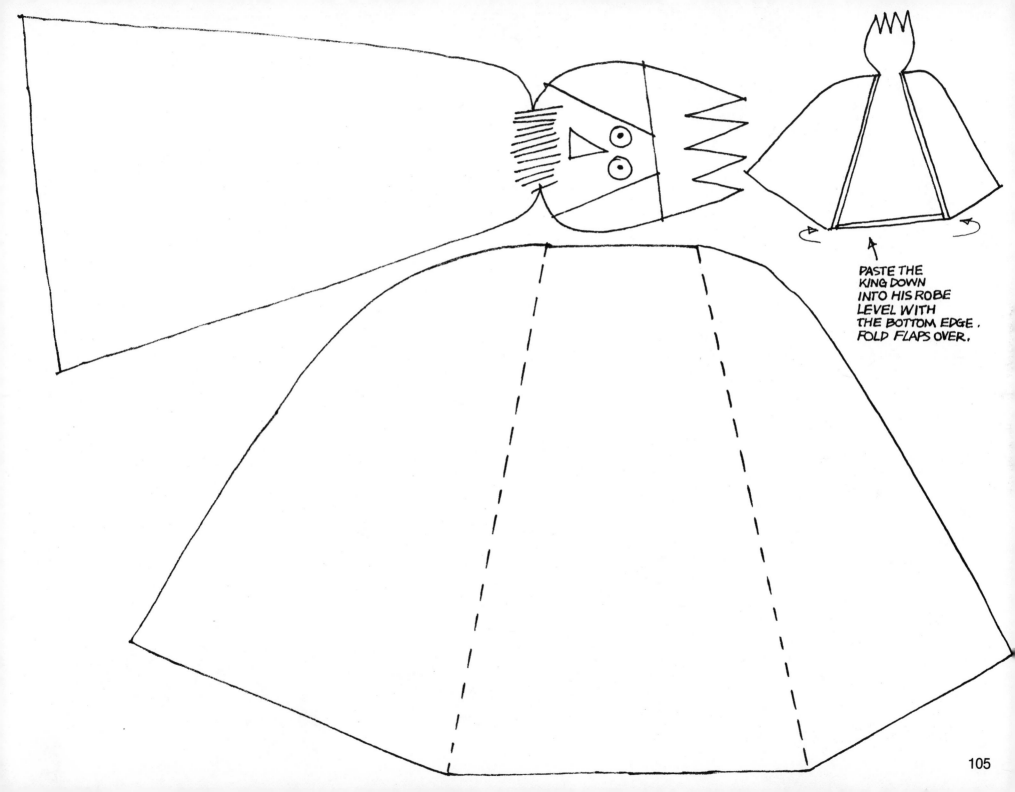

PASTE THE
KING DOWN
INTO HIS ROBE
LEVEL WITH
THE BOTTOM EDGE.
FOLD FLAPS OVER.

105

YOU'LL NEVER BELIEVE WHAT I SAW!

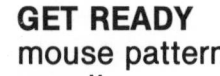

GET READY
mouse pattern for a "write-on"
pencil
crayons
scissors
white typing paper

GET SET
1. Trace the pattern on this page to make a mouse-shaped "write-on." Use sturdy white typing paper.
2. Cut out and fold on the dotted line. Then color the mouse.
3. On the back side, begin a story with this sentence: "You'll never believe what I saw!"

GO
Then pretend you are a tiny mouse who sat very near where your Bible story for this week OR any favorite Bible story took place. Tell how the story happened as it might have looked to you (the mouse). Be careful not to get run over by a camel or a chariot or become a meal for a lion! And don't let anyone pitch a tent or build an altar on your tail!

the CREATION CONNECTION

Any Bible story

THE GOOD EGG

(On the egg: BE KIND / READ GOD'S WORD / LOVE ONE ANOTHER / PRAY WITHOUT CEASING / FLEE FROM EVIL / SPEAK THE TRUTH)

(Speech bubble: NOW, TURN THE TWO HALVES UNTIL YOU CAN READ A SPECIAL MESSAGE!)

GET READY
a L'Eggs stocking egg
permanent felt-tip pen

GET SET
1. Use your pen to write these words around the edge of one half of your egg. Write them in the order they appear here, and space them about 1½ inches apart. (Some eggs have tiny notches about 1½ inches apart. Write one word by each notch.)

2. On the other half of your egg, use exactly the same spacing to write these words in this order.

GO
Put the two halves of your egg together. Twist them until you are able to read six good rules to live by.

the CREATION CONNECTION
Any brief, simple rules for Christian living
Scripture verses and references (drill or practice)
The Ten Commandments

WE DO WINDOWS

GET READY

scrap paper and pencil
colored chalk and water
damp cloth or paper towel
newspaper
a window

GET SET

1. Choose a window that can be reached easily and one on which you can get permission to create a chalk drawing. (Be sure to promise to clean the window when your drawing comes off!)
2. Choose a scene from your favorite Bible story to recreate in a drawing. Sketch your idea with pencil on scrap paper about the same size as the window you are using.
3. Then use wet chalk to draw a picture on the glass OR cover the entire window with a thick coat of wet chalk and do a finger painting.

GO

Enjoy the chalk painting(s) just as long as you wish; then just wipe off the chalk with a damp cloth or paper towel. Rub the window sparkling clean with a piece of newspaper. (Be sure to clean up the chalk dust on the sill and floor too!)

REMEMBER PEOPLE WILL SEE YOUR PICTURE FROM THE OUTSIDE TOO!

COLORED CHALK

The CREATION CONNECTION

Any Bible story or concept

Gifts for a sick friend

GET READY

a heavyweight cardboard box (at least 16" long)

an adult helper with a sharp cutting tool

a plastic cup

small box of Kleenex

one or more flowers, real or artificial

a small, flat box (such as a cigar box)

plastic or foil tray (optional)

collection of small work tools and toys (such as crayons, pencils, toy figures, finger puppets, tiny books, cards, etc.)

paper bag

safety pins or decorated diaper pins

clear tape

GET SET

1. Ask someone to help you cut from a heavy cardboard box a tray table like the one on this page.

2. Glue a plastic or foil tray to the top of the table.

3. Add a plastic cup full of flowers, a small box of Kleenex and a small surprise box of work tools and toys. Glue all these in place on the tray table.

4. Make a bed-wastebasket! Decorate a strong, medium-size paper bag with a cheerful picture or design. Reinforce with a strip of clear tape around the top edge to avoid tearing. Add safety pins or decorated diaper pins to use in attaching the bag to the mattress at the side of the bed.

GO

Take these special gifts to a friend who is sick and must stay in bed for awhile. You might also share some of your very own books, the Sunday school papers from the weeks your friend has missed, and a cheerful smile!

the CREATION CONNECTION

Caring

"A merry heart doeth good like a medicine" (Prov. 17:22)

Helping others

WINDOW JUNGLE

GET READY
several natural sponges
parsley, mustard, bean
sprout seeds
string
tacks, hammer

GET SET
1. Soak the sponges in water.
2. Squeeze lightly, so they are not dripping.
3. Poke seeds into the holes in the sponges.
4. Tie string around, or use a needle to pull string through each sponge.
5. Hang in front of a window.
6. Keep sponges moist at all times.

GO
Watch your jungle grow! (It will take a week or more to grow enough greens for a sandwich or salad topping.)

ME TARZAN YOU JANE!

BUG OFF BEE. I'M BUSY!

WHATCHA DOIN, MARY KAY?

I'M GONNA GROW A JUNGLE ON THIS ITSY, TEENY, BITTY SPONGE

the CREATION CONNECTION
Growth
Nature
gift idea for Mom or sick friend

A Rainbow of Promises

GET READY

Colored paper (all rainbow colors)
String or yarn
Magazine pictures, crayons
Scissors and paste
A list of favorite Bible promises

GET SET

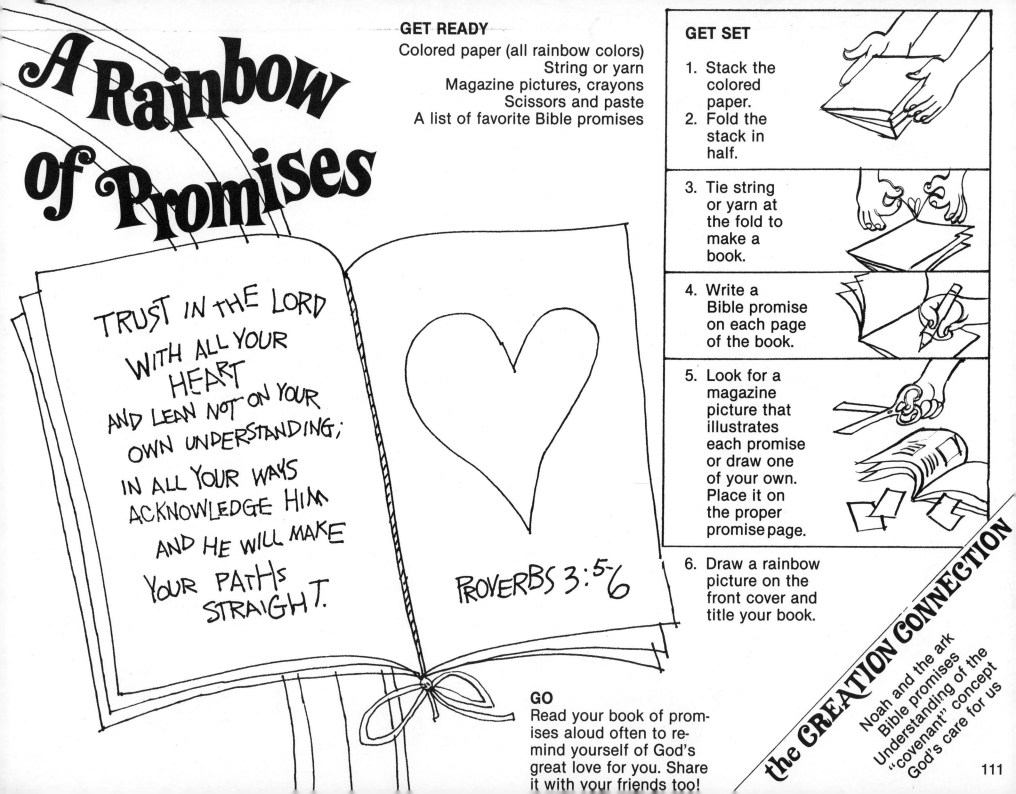

1. Stack the colored paper.
2. Fold the stack in half.

3. Tie string or yarn at the fold to make a book.

4. Write a Bible promise on each page of the book.

5. Look for a magazine picture that illustrates each promise or draw one of your own. Place it on the proper promise page.

6. Draw a rainbow picture on the front cover and title your book.

TRUST IN THE LORD WITH ALL YOUR HEART AND LEAN NOT ON YOUR OWN UNDERSTANDING; IN ALL YOUR WAYS ACKNOWLEDGE HIM AND HE WILL MAKE YOUR PATHS STRAIGHT.

PROVERBS 3:5-6

GO

Read your book of promises aloud often to remind yourself of God's great love for you. Share it with your friends too!

the CREATION CONNECTION

Noah and the ark
Bible promises
Understanding of the "covenant" concept
God's care for us

111

PORT-A-STORY BOARD

DOES ANYBODY WANT TO HEAR A BIBLE STORY?

YES!

PORT-A-STORY BOARD

GET READY
a flat gift box with a cover (at least 9"x12")
a piece of felt as large as the box cover
felt scraps of various colors
felt-tip pens
patterns (see the pattern section of this book)
wide ribbon or elastic
Velcro tabs or small pieces of Velcro fastening tape
paper and glue

GET SET
1. Cut the large piece of felt to fit exactly inside the cover of the box.
2. Glue it carefully in place.
3. Use the shapes in the pattern section of this book or draw shapes of your own to make the felt characters for your favorite Bible story or stories.
4. Use felt-tip pens to fill in faces, clothes, and other details on your characters.
5. Place your characters in the bottom of the box.
6. Decorate the cover of your box. (You might want to write _____ 's STORYBOARD.)
7. Use a wide ribbon to make a "belt" and "handle" on your portable story board.

GO
Use your story board to show and tell your favorite stories to your friends — at church, at home, at school, on a trip or a picnic. It can go anywhere you can go!

PORT-A-STORY BOARD

The CREATION CONNECTION

Any Bible story that can be illustrated

THE MIRACLE OF MAN

"And the Lord God formed man of the dust of the ground, and breathed into his nostrils the breath of life; and man became a living soul" (Gen. 2:7).

GET READY
An inked stamp pad OR thick felt-tip pen
a large piece of poster board

GET SET
You often hear that all men are created equal. Do you believe that is true? We do know that all men are different—no two are exactly alike. Prove it for yourself with this activity.

Use your ink pad or felt-tip pen and posterboard to collect as many fingerprints, hand prints, and foot-prints as you can squeeze on your posterboard. (If you're using pen, you must rub it lightly across the person's finger, hand, or foot and make the print quickly while the ink is still damp.)

GO
Observe your collection of prints. Are any two exactly the same? Are you glad?

the **CREATION CONNECTION**
Considering the equalities and inequalities of man
God's creative genius

113

The Fifth Day of Creation

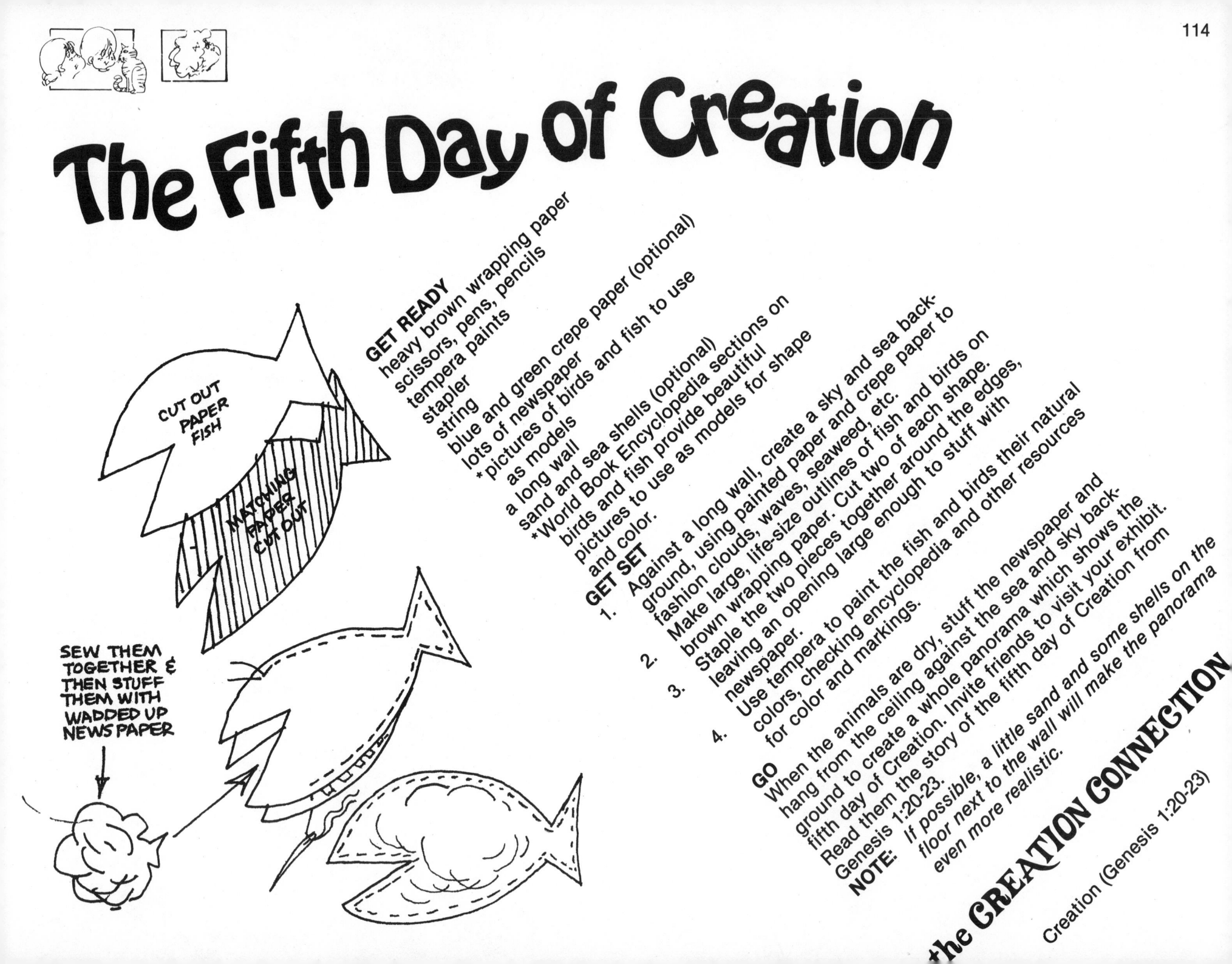

CUT OUT PAPER FISH

MATCHING PAPER CUT OUT

SEW THEM TOGETHER & THEN STUFF THEM WITH WADDED UP NEWS PAPER

GET READY
heavy brown wrapping paper
scissors, pens, pencils
tempera paints
stapler
string
blue and green crepe paper (optional)
lots of newspaper
* pictures of birds and fish to use as models
a long wall
sand and sea shells (optional)

*World Book Encyclopedia sections on birds and fish provide beautiful pictures to use as models for shape and color.

GET SET
1. Against a long wall, create a sky and sea background, using painted paper and crepe paper to fashion clouds, waves, seaweed, etc.
2. Make large, life-size outlines of fish and birds on brown wrapping paper. Cut two of each shape. Staple the two pieces together around the edges, leaving an opening large enough to stuff with newspaper.
3. Use tempera to paint the fish and birds their natural colors, checking encyclopedia and other resources for color and markings.
4. When the animals are dry, stuff the newspaper and hang from the ceiling against the sea and sky background to create a whole panorama which shows the fifth day of Creation. Invite friends to visit your exhibit. Read them the story of the fifth day of Creation from Genesis 1:20-23.

NOTE: *If possible, a little sand and some shells on the floor next to the wall will make the panorama even more realistic.*

the CREATION CONNECTION

Creation (Genesis 1:20-23)

115

INVITE NOAH'S ZOO TO LUNCH!

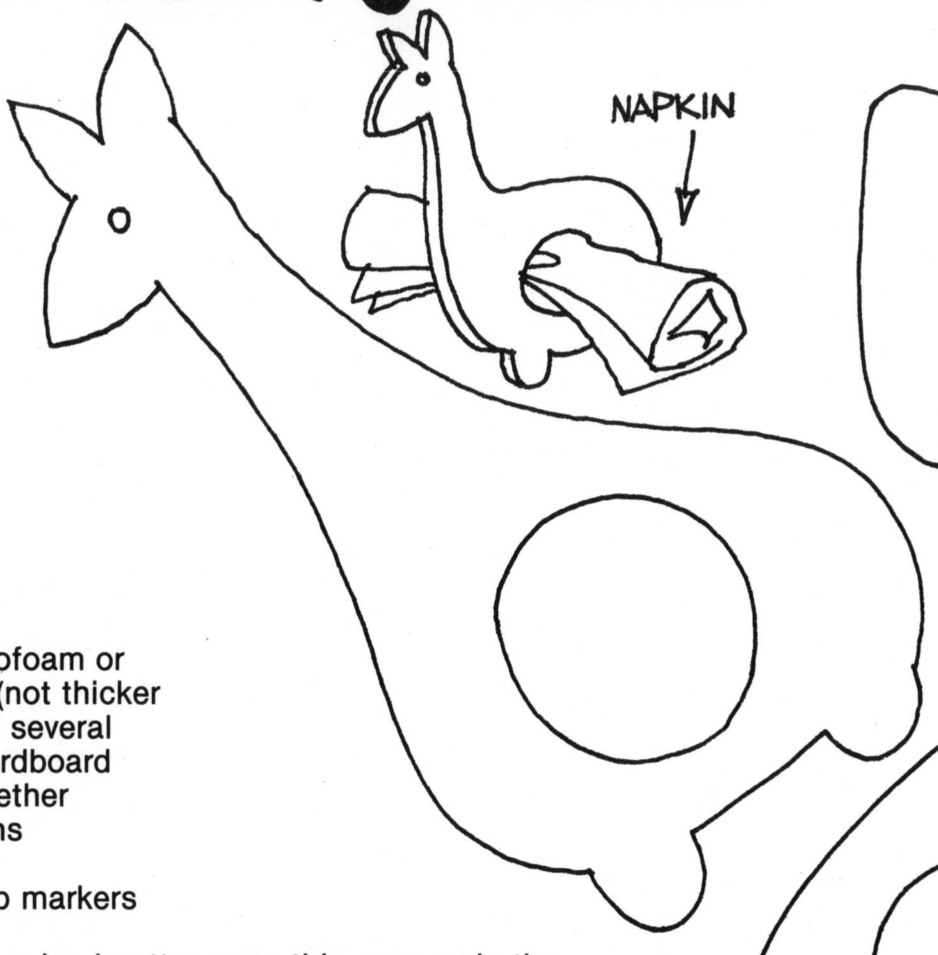

NAPKIN

GET READY
blocks of styrofoam or
    balsawood (not thicker
    than 1") OR several
    layers of cardboard
    bonded together
animal patterns
knife
paint or felt-tip markers

GET SET
1. Trace the animal patterns on this page or in the pattern section of this book to draw animal shapes on the foam, wood, or cardboard surface.
2. Use a dull knife to cut out the shapes. Then draw a one-and-a-half to two-inch circle in the center of each animal and cut out the circles.

GO
Presto! You have Noah's zoo ready for lunch ... as *napkin rings!* Make one for each member of your family—plus an extra one or two for guests. (Add eyes and other details with paint or pen, if you like.)

the CREATION CONNECTION

Noah's ark
Bible animals

the CREATION CONNECTION

Red Sea Crossing (Exodus 14)
Storm at Sea (Matthew 14:24-33)
Any "sea" story

GO

Paint over the wavy stripes of color. Your wax drawing, making four or more wavy stripes to show through the painted stripes to make an attractive picture.

GET SET

1. Think of a Bible story that takes place on or near a sea or ocean.
2. Draw, with very light pencil, a picture to illustrate that one story.
3. Shave a candle so that one end has a sharp point for drawing.
4. Trace over the pencil lines with the candle. Press hard to make thick wax lines.
5. Mix four or five different colors of thin paint.

GET READY

pencil
white or Manila construction paper
an old candle
4 colors of paint (tempera)

wax'n waves

BIG-MOUTH PUPPETS

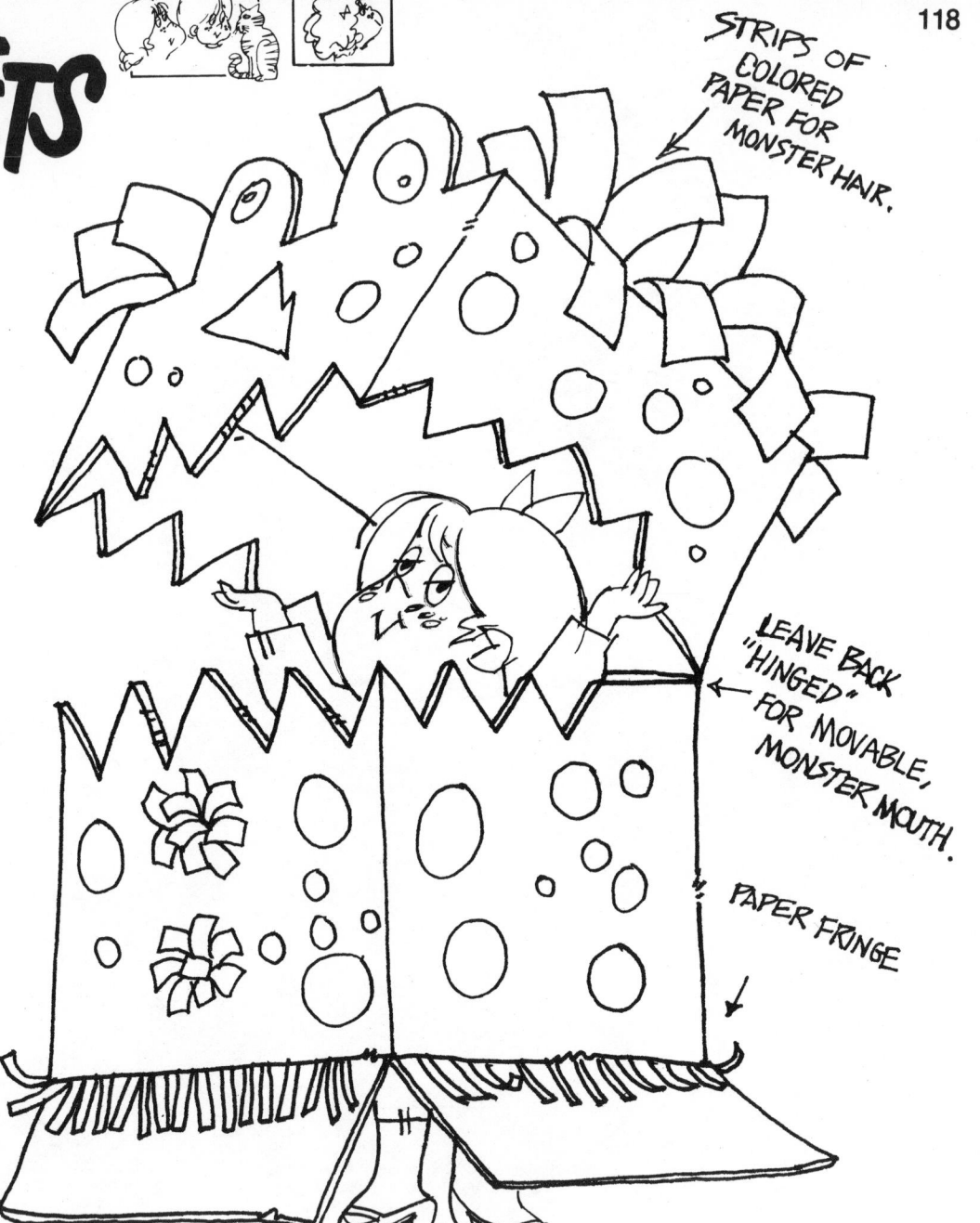

STRIPS OF COLORED PAPER FOR MONSTER HAIR.

LEAVE BACK "HINGED" FOR MOVABLE, MONSTER MOUTH.

PAPER FRINGE

GET READY

sturdy cardboard box (as deep as from the top of your head to your waist), scraps of fabric, yarn, colored paper, contact paper, newspaper, junk items such as tin cans, hangers, small plastic containers, lids, etc.

paint

large paint brushes

glue and/or stapler

scissors

a picture OR your own drawing of a "horrible" monster

a knife (ask a grownup to help you with this)

GET SET

1. Ask a grownup to help you cut a mouth with jagged teeth along three sides of your box (as shown).
2. Cut two large half-circles in the top of the box at the front edge. Bend these half-circles up to make eyes.
3. Paint your box with stripes, polka dots, or wild splotches of color.
4. Add hair, ears, eyeballs, nose, antennae, etc., with scraps and junk.

GO

Get inside your monster. Pretend you are a life-size "Muppet" and give your own one-man show. Sing your favorite songs, tell a story, do a ventriloquist act with a friend, OR get together with a group of friends who have also created "monsters" and act out the words to "The Monster Song" on this page. (A whole group of kids could do the song as a choral reading.) Use your gravelly voice to make it scary.

Deep in a cave of the human heart
Is a monsters' lair, all grimy 'n dark.

*And if for just a moment, you forget what you're
    about*
*And open up that door a crack, there's hardly any
    doubt*
The monsters'll get 'cha — Oh, ya' better watch out!
The monsters'll get 'cha — Oh, ya' better watch out!

GRISLY GREED with his grabby claws
Snatches what he catches for his juicy jaws
And JADED OLE JEALOUSY comes creepin' 'cross
    the floor
To make you hate what you loved before.

ARROGANT EGO with his capital I's
Leers from behind his "humble" disguise
While OLD TYRANT TEMPER lurks behind your back
And watches his chance for a sneak attack!

REFRAIN: *Oh, if for just a moment, you forget what
            you're about
        And open up that door a crack, there's
            hardly any doubt
        The monsters'll get 'cha — Oh, ya'
        better watch out!
        The monsters'll get 'cha — Oh, ya'
        better watch out!*

(whisper)
High in the corner, way out of the light
Is a nest of widow spiders, some black, some white ...
LIES they are, who spin a web so taut
That the tiniest of them will get you hopelessly
    caught!

(explosively)
Danger! DISHONESTY! He'll hypnotize your mind,
Make the bad look good and the cruel, kind,
He bribes behavior with temptations sweet
Then he's got 'cha! Get a mirror and take a look at a
    cheat!

THE MONSTER SONG

*Oh, if for just a moment, you forget what
    you're about And open up that door a
crack, there's hardly any doubt
The monsters'll get 'cha — Oh, ya' better watch out!
The monsters'll get 'cha — Oh, ya' better watch out!*

It's when you least suspect it that you begin to see
Those monsters stealin' in to make YOU their tasty
    meal
Don't mess with them; their temper is impossible to
    tame
And you know that if they get you, there's no one else
    to blame.
Roll a great, humongous stone into the door of that
    cave
And block it once forever — Don't pretend to be brave
But arm yourself with the Truth of God's Word
And run to where those monster voices can't be
    heard!

REFRAIN: *'Cuz if for just a moment, you forget
            what you're about
        And open up that door a crack, There's
            hardly any doubt
        The monsters'll get 'cha — Oh, ya'
        better watch out!
        The monsters'll get 'cha — Oh, ya'
        better watch out!*

the CREATION CONNECTION
Lessons in the control of jealousy,
hate, greed, lying, etc.
Song-leading
Story-telling

GET READY

a cereal box
construction paper (gray)
scissors
paste

felt-tip pen
story lists (below)
Zip-loc bags (4)

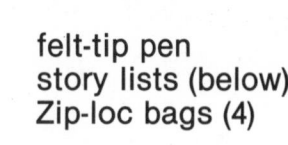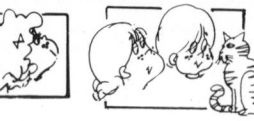

GET SET

1. Use the elephant pattern and the pictures on this page to make a very hungry elephant.
2. Cover the front side of the box with gray construction paper.
3. Paste the mouth part of the lower half on the box and cut a hole as shown.
4. Attach the elephant head and trunk at the top of the box so that it hangs down to cover the hole, but can be lifted to "feed" peanuts into the mouth.
5. Trace the peanut pattern to make thirty-two peanuts. Separate the peanuts into four groups of eight. Write the eight words from the DANIEL story on eight peanuts and put them in a Zip-loc bag.
   Follow the same procedure for each of the other three groups of story words.

GO

Play a game with a group of small children. First tell them the four stories if they are not already familiar with them. (DANIEL IN THE LIONS' DEN ... DAVID AND GOLIATH ... ELIJAH AND THE WIDOW ... NOAH'S ARK) As you review each story, explain to the children that you will give them a bag of peanuts. They must "read" each peanut (with your help). If the word on the peanut is associated with the story, it is a good peanut, and they may feed it to the elephant.

If the peanut bears a word that is NOT associated with the story, they may throw it on the floor and say "Rotten Peanut!" What fun they will have feeding the elephant and throwing away rotten peanuts. Do just one story at a time and enjoy each one with your young friends.

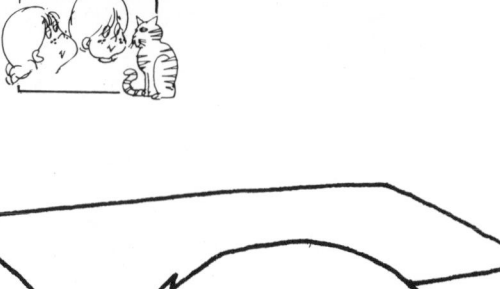

THIS IS A GREAT GAME TO PLAY WITH SMALL CHILDREN!

FEED THE ELEPHANT

the CREATION CONNECTION

Daniel in the Lions' Den
David and Goliath
Elijah and the widow
Noah's Ark
Any Bible story

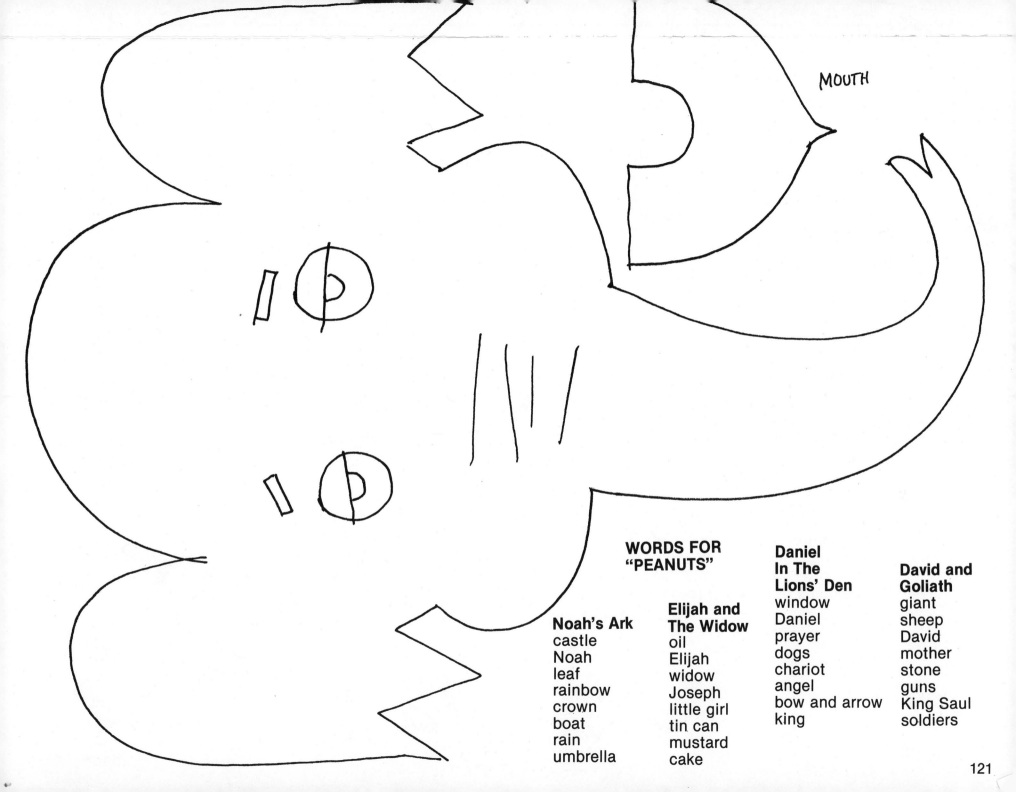

MOUTH

WORDS FOR "PEANUTS"

Noah's Ark
castle
Noah
leaf
rainbow
crown
boat
rain
umbrella

Elijah and The Widow
oil
Elijah
widow
Joseph
little girl
tin can
mustard
cake

Daniel In The Lions' Den
window
Daniel
prayer
dogs
chariot
angel
bow and arrow
king

David and Goliath
giant
sheep
David
mother
stone
guns
King Saul
soldiers

121

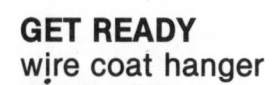

LET THERE BE LIGHT!

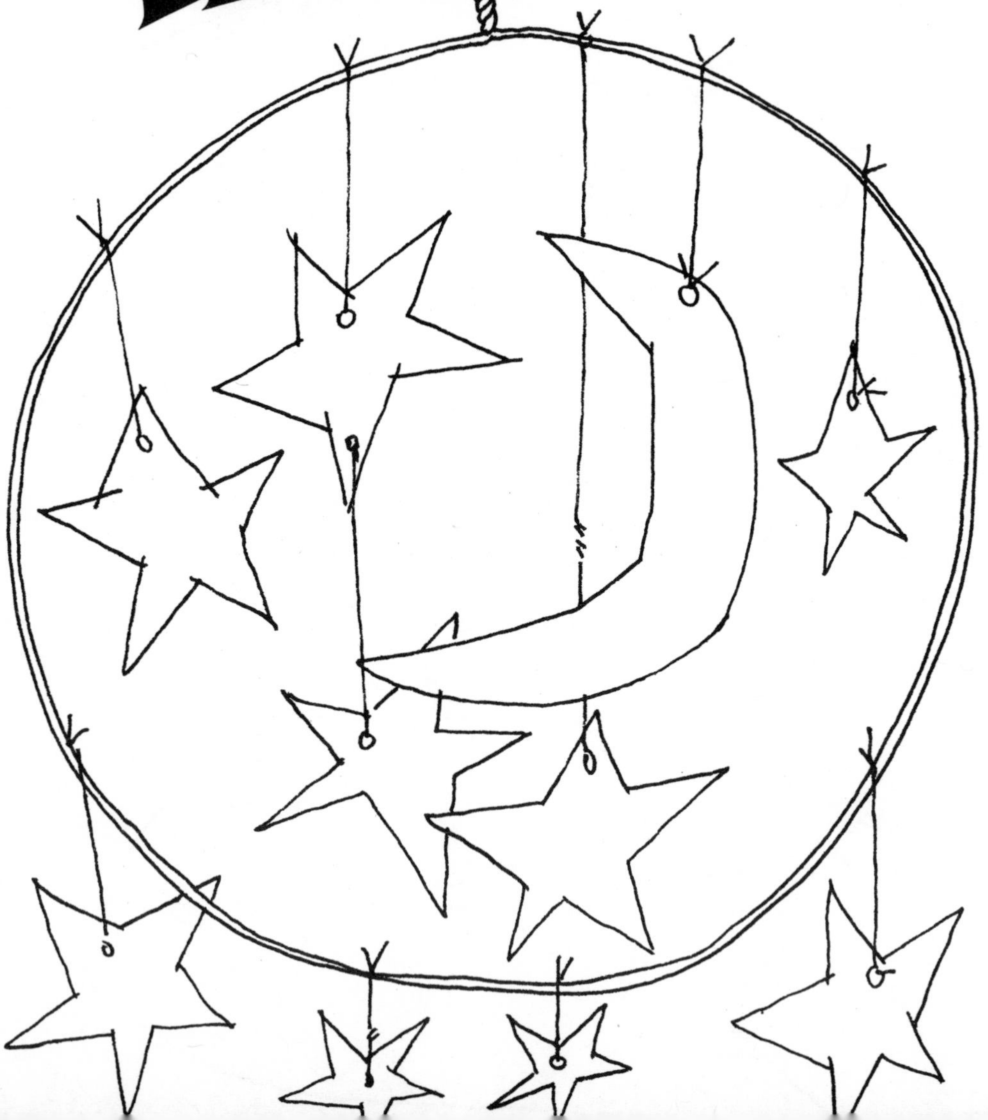

GET READY
wire coat hanger
plastic lids
scissors
a paper punch
string
yellow permanent felt-tip pen

GET SET
1. Bend a coat hanger into a circle to represent the sun.
2. Cut from plastic container lids one moon shape and many star shapes. (See patterns on this page.) Color them yellow on both sides with a permanent felt-tip marker.
3. Punch a hole in each star and moon. Tie them to the hanger with varying lengths of string.

GO
Hang your mobile in a place where a breeze can blow it. As you watch it move, thank God for making the sun, moon, and stars.

I'M MAKIN' A MOBILE OUT OF A WIRE COAT HANGER

PATTERNS

IS IT NIGHT TIME ALREADY?

the CREATION CONNECTION

Creation
Genesis 1

MAP IN A BOX

GET READY
salt dough (2 cups salt,
 2 cups flour,
 1⅓ cups water)
a cardboard box lid
tempera paints
brushes
felt-tip pens
toothpicks and paper scraps

GET SET
1. Make salt dough by mixing the salt and flour, then slowly adding the water and stirring together until smooth.
2. Spread the mixture onto the box lid.
3. With your hands, make a relief map by building up hills and mountains, pressing out flat areas for lowlands and oceans, making paths for rivers or major roads.
4. Use toothpicks and paper scraps to make tiny flags to use as markers in labeling cities and major landmarks.
5. After your map has dried, paint the land and water areas.

GO
Use your map as an aid in retelling a Bible story or event.

MT. EBAL
MT. GERIZIM
SHECHEM
SAMARIA
KANGU RIVER

FLOUR

the CREATION CONNECTION
Journey of Mary and Joseph from Nazareth to Bethlehem
Paul's missionary journeys
The Holy Land during a specific time in history
Creation story (third day)
The Exodus

SAND PAINTING

WHITE SAND

WHITE SAND FOR EYE

LIGHT BROWN SAND

LIGHT BLUE SAND

DARK BROWN SAND

GET READY
sand
food coloring
small glass jars or plastic
  containers with lids
white glue, small brush
a piece of cardboard
paper cup or tin can

GET SET
1. If you are using sea sand, you must first "wash" it by rinsing it several times with clear water. Then spread it out to dry.
2. Put a portion of sand in several jars. Add a different color of food coloring to each jar. Shake the jar until the sand is completely colored. (Keep adding food coloring until the color is a little darker than you want it to be when finished—it will dry a lighter color.)
3. Pour the sand out on newspaper to dry. Then store the dry sand in the same jars.
4. On a large piece of cardboard, draw a picture or design related to one of your favorite Bible stories. Plan to use only a few colors of sand, and make figures large and simple.
5. Decide what color you will make each part. Thin white glue with a little water in a paper cup or tin can.
6. Paint one section of your drawing with the glue mixtures and sprinkle one color of sand on that part. Let it dry and shake off the excess sand.
7. Use the same procedure to color the other parts of your drawing . . . one color at a time.

GO
When you are finished, you will have a lovely sand painting.

the CREATION CONNECTION
Any Bible story or object

Checking Out Solar Energy

I. Checking Out Solar Energy

GET READY
3 cans of the same size
black and white paint
   (very thick tempera OR
   latex)
water
thermometer
sun

GET SET
1. Remove labels from all the cans.
2. Paint one can white, one can black, and leave one plain.
3. Fill each can with the same amount of water.
4. Place all three cans together in a sunny spot for two to three hours.

GO
Use the thermometer to check the water temperature in each can. Which can is the best solar heater? Do you know why?

WHEW! IT'S HOT ON THIS PAGE!

THINK I'LL PUT ON A PAIR OF SHORTS!

SUN POWER!

Sun Fun

II. Sun Fun

GET READY 
a wall in the shade
2-4 players, each with a
   small mirror
sun

GET SET
1.   Players should practice holding their mirrors so
     that they can catch the rays of the sun and reflect
     sunlight on the shaded wall. Make the spots of
     sun move all over the wall.
2.   Appoint one player to be IT.

GO
IT chases the other sunspots around on the wall, try-
ing to tag them with his spot. When he has "caught"
them all, someone else is IT! (Choose one area of the
wall that is a *resting* place for sunspots ... where IT
cannot go. Only one spot at a time may rest there.)

SUN POWER!

More Sun Fun

III. More Sun Fun

GET READY
balloon (3 for each
   player)
magnifying glasses (1 for
   each player)
tacks or tape
sun
GET SET
1. Blow up all the balloons to the same size and
    tape or tack the neck of three balloons for each
    player to a wall or fence.
2. All contestants must get their magnifying glasses
    ready ... say GO!

GO
Each player must hold his magnifying glass to make a
steady spot of sunlight on the surface of a balloon.
(The smaller and steadier the spot, the hotter it is and
the faster it will burst the balloon.) See who can burst
all three balloons first to win the race.

IT'S SO·O·O·O PEACEFUL & QUIET HERE!

SUN POWER!

Measuring with the Sun

ZOWIE! THAT TREE IS 80 FEET TALL!

WOW! AND YOU MEASURED HOW LONG THE SHADOW WAS TO FIND THAT OUT!

IV. Measuring with the Sun

GET READY
2 12" rulers
paper and pencil
sun

GET SET
1. Choose a tall object you want to measure (such as a tree or building).
2. Stand one ruler straight on end on the ground near to the object you are measuring.
3. Measure the ruler's shadow with the other ruler and record the number of *inches.*
4. Now, measure the shadow of the tall object to find out how many *feet* long it is.

GO
Multiply the length of the tall object's shadow by 12. Then divide the number you get by the length of the ruler's shadow. That will tell you the height of the tall object in *feet.* Aren't you clever???? Think how much MORE clever God had to be to create the sun!

WONDER HOW LONG IT IS 'TIL DINNER TIME?!

the **CREATION CONNECTION**
Introducing the idea of Christian responsibility in energy conservation
Praising God for sunlight
Recognizing solar resources

129

GET READY

a small pumpkin
a plastic container (such as
  cottage cheese carton or
  Cool Whip container
pebbles, sand, or floral foam
flowers and/or waxed leaves

GET SET

1. Cut a hole in the top of the pumpkin and hollow it out.
2. Fill a plastic container with pebbles, sand, or floral foam and set it down inside the pumpkin.
3. Arrange fall cut flowers, wild or dried flowers, and/or waxed leaves in the container.

GO

PRESTO! You have a lovely fall centerpiece for a dinner or party table. Thank God for leaves and flowers ... and pumpkins too! (Dry the pumpkin seeds, salt, and bake them. They're yummy!)

SMALL CHRISTMAS ORNAMENTS

PUMPKIN

A Harvest Centerpiece

the CREATION CONNECTION

Harvest time
Thanksgiving

MATZO & HAROSETH FOR PASSOVER

GET READY

For Matzo
3½ cups flour
1 cup water
rolling pin
shortening
  (to grease cookie sheet)
cookie sheet
fork and knife
oven

For Haroseth
1 cup chopped apples
¼ cup chopped nuts
1 teaspoon cinnamon
2 tablespoons grape
  juice

GET SET

1. Mix and knead flour and water and roll out very thin on a generously floured surface.
2. Lift carefully onto a greased cookie sheet and prick all over with a fork; then score into small squares with a knife.
3. Bake at 475 degrees for 10-15 minutes or until browned lightly.
4. To make Haroseth, mix apples, nuts, cinnamon, and grape juice together, and set aside to spread on the matzo when it is done.

GO

Locate a book in which you can read the story of Passover and the Seder. Enjoy your homemade matzo and haroseth as you read.

You don't have to be Jewish to celebrate Passover. Passover is the Festival of Freedom, when people all over the world remember the exodus of the Hebrews from Egypt after 430 years of living under the rule of cruel kings.

The Seder is a traditional family dinner — something like a special kind of Thanksgiving dinner — which commemorates the Passover events and the beginning of spring with special foods, songs, and prayers.

Matzo bread is an important part of the meal because it reminds us of the hard times the Hebrew people suffered while on their long journey from Egypt.

the CREATION CONNECTION

Passover

131

GET READY

Sturdy paper or styrofoam milk shake-size glass with plastic lid (Buy a milk shake at McDonalds or Baskin-Robbins and drink it to get one!)
scissors
2 pipe cleaners
tempera paints (mixed with detergent)
paper punch

GET SET

1. Trace the head pattern from this page on the plastic lid and cut it out.

·2. Cut a slit in the center of the bottom of the glass. Fold in the points at the bottom of the turkey neck and insert in the slit; then open the points to hold the head in place.

PATTERN
TO FOLLOW FOR
LID CUT OUT

TAB

TAB

3   Cut three-inch deep slits at even spaces in the top of the glass and bend the pieces back to form feathers. Cut off the bottom two feathers.

4. Make two holes in the bottom of the turkey. Twist two pipe cleaners together to make one long one. Poke the ends through the holes from the inside to make feet. Bend the pipe cleaners to make two three-toed feet.

GO

Paint your turkey and enjoy him as your Thanksgiving centerpiece or individual favor. (Smaller turkeys for individual favors can be made in the same way by using small paper cups.)

MAKE A MENORAH FOR CHANUKAH

The story of Chanukah as the eight-day Festival of Lights is a wonderful traditional story of a real miracle. The hero of the story is Judas Maccabaeus. Find and read the story in a library book or encyclopedia. Then you will enjoy so much more making this menorah which is the symbol of the Chanukah story.

GET READY

very stiff paper, tag or lightweight
  cardboard (about 9 x 12)
scissors
yellow construction paper
glue
ruler, pencil

GET SET

1. Use your ruler to divide your paper into three equal sections as shown.
2. Then mark off a very narrow piece of the third section. This will be your tab for gluing the piece together.
3. Fold the *first* or *top* section down evenly over the *second* or *middle* section and press firmly on the fold.
4. Now make eighteen evenly spaced, parallel cuts halfway into the two folded sections as pictured to make candles.
5. Fold and glue the tab in place as shown to make the piece stand.
6. Invert every other "candle" by folding it down into the base as shown. You should then have nine candles standing.
7. Cut nine flames from yellow construction paper and glue one to the top of each candle.

WHAT'S A CHON·NU·KA?

IT'S PRONOUNCED "HONIKA" AND IT'S A JEWISH HOLIDAY!

GO

Share your menorah and the story of Chankuah with friends and family. If you wish, you may attach a "flame" to the center candle only and use your menorah during the Chanukah celebration, adding a "flame" for each day of the Festival of Lights.

The CREATION CONNECTION

Chanukah

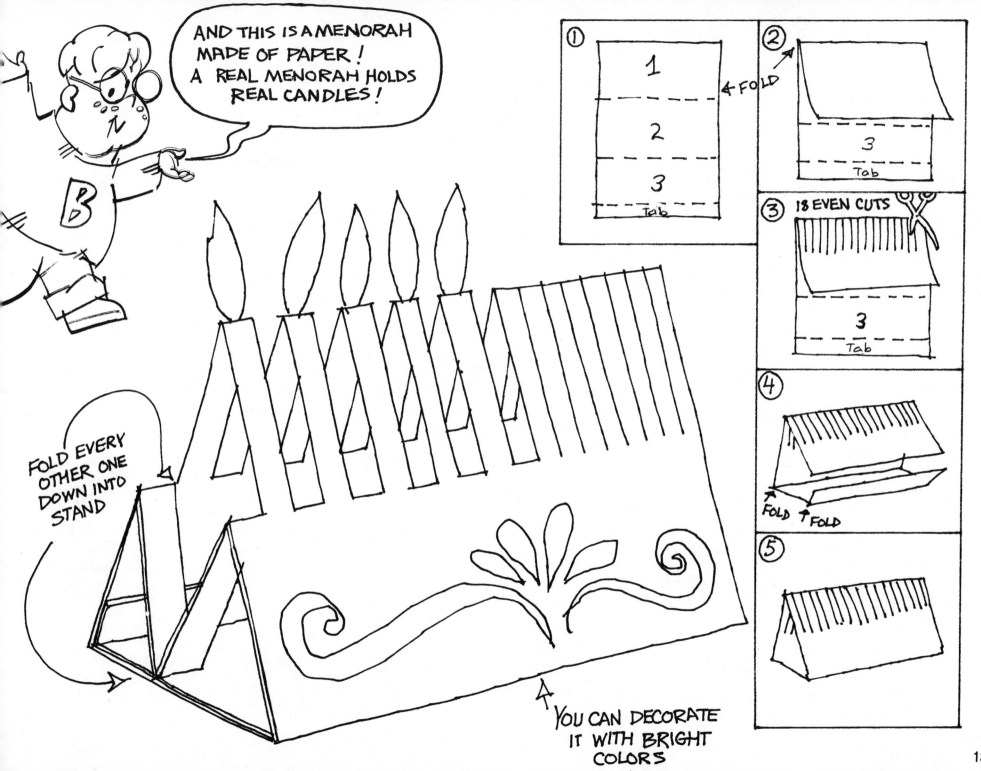

AND THIS IS A MENORAH MADE OF PAPER! A REAL MENORAH HOLDS REAL CANDLES!

① 1 2 3 Tab ← FOLD

② 3 Tab

③ 18 EVEN CUTS 3 Tab

④ FOLD FOLD

⑤

FOLD EVERY OTHER ONE DOWN INTO STAND

YOU CAN DECORATE IT WITH BRIGHT COLORS

STAR OF DAVID

GET READY
heavy colored paper
ruler
scissors
pencil
glue or tape
paper punch, string or
  yarn

GET SET
1. Cut twelve long, narrow strips of paper, all the same size.
2. Mark off a small section at the end of each strip. This part will be the "tab."

   Use your ruler and pencil to divide the remaining part of each strip into three equal sections.

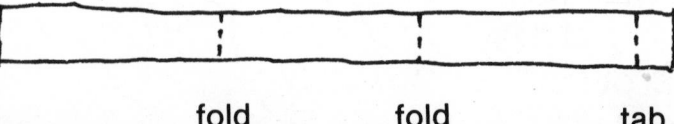

fold   fold   tab

3. Fold on the marks and make each strip into a triangle. Glue or tape the tab.

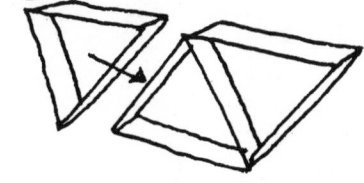

4. Now glue three triangles together to make a row of triangles.

   Repeat to get another row of three triangles.

5. Now glue the two rows together as shown. This will make a six-sided figure.

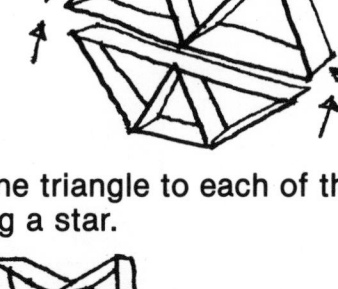

6. Glue one triangle to each of the six sides, creating a star.

GO
Punch a hole in the top part of the star and string a loop of string or yarn through for hanging.

The CREATION CONNECTION
Chanukah, Christmas

ADVENT WREATH

GET READY

Play clay (see recipe section)
Four candles
Small clips of evergreen branches
  OR green toothpicks
Ribbons or yarns in red and gold
  colors
Green paint (optional)
Straight pins or wide masking tape
Plastic sandwich bags

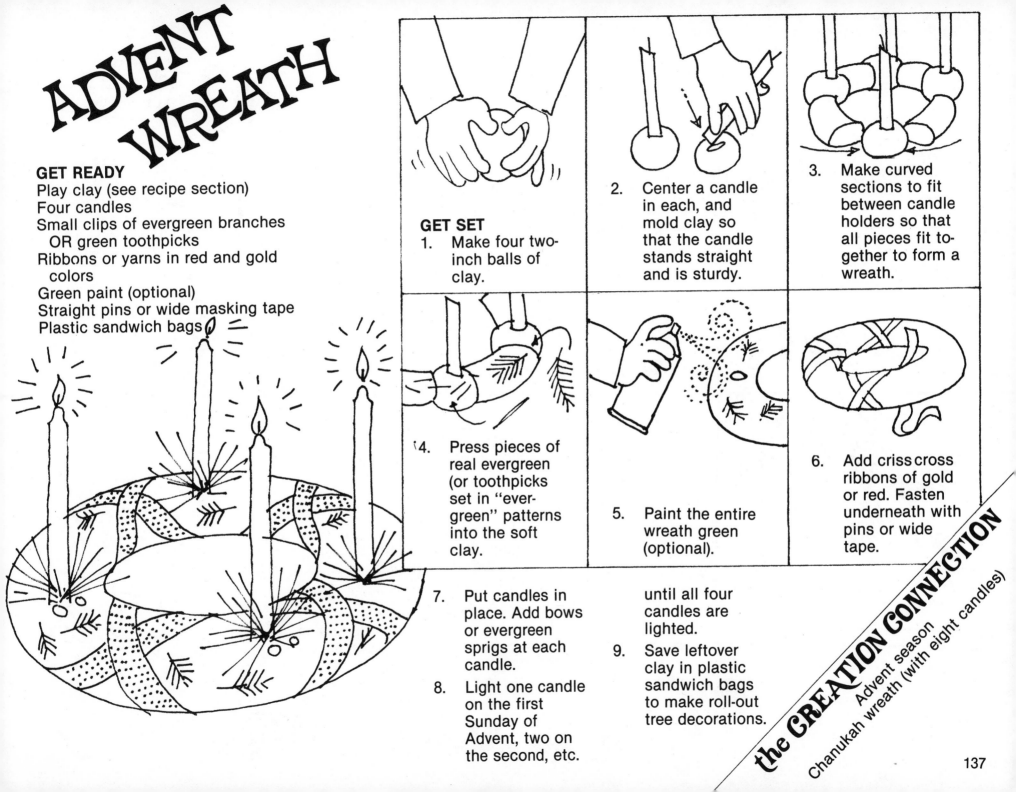

GET SET

1. Make four two-inch balls of clay.

2. Center a candle in each, and mold clay so that the candle stands straight and is sturdy.

3. Make curved sections to fit between candle holders so that all pieces fit together to form a wreath.

4. Press pieces of real evergreen (or toothpicks set in "evergreen" patterns into the soft clay.

5. Paint the entire wreath green (optional).

6. Add criss cross ribbons of gold or red. Fasten underneath with pins or wide tape.

7. Put candles in place. Add bows or evergreen sprigs at each candle.

8. Light one candle on the first Sunday of Advent, two on the second, etc. until all four candles are lighted.

9. Save leftover clay in plastic sandwich bags to make roll-out tree decorations.

the CREATION CONNECTION
Advent season
Chanukah wreath (with eight candles)

137

Three Advent Calendars

The idea of an Advent calendar is that every day from the 1st of December to the 25th, you open one part of the calendar. Therefore, an Advent calendar must have 25 surprise parts.

GET READY

Calendar I

construction paper
lots of old Christmas cards
scissors, glue, felt-tip pens, crayons
tape or pins
25 Scripture verses related to the Nativity

Calendar II

a large piece of solid-colored fabric
felt (in a contrasting color)
needle and thread, OR fabric glue
candy
25 Scripture verses related to Love and Peace, each written on a small card or strip of paper

Calendar III

lots of old Christmas cards
cardboard (poster-size)
glue, scissors, felt-tip pen

GET SET

Calendar I

Make 25 decorated Christmas folders. Tape them on a wall or door or pin them on a curtain in the shape of a tree. Write a Nativity-related Scripture verse inside each folder.

Calendar II
Danish Klockasträng

Sew felt heart-shaped pockets on a large piece of material. Tuck a piece of candy and a Scripture verse in each pocket.

Calendar III

Make 25 windows in a large poster. Paste tiny pictures from old Christmas cards on a second poster underneath each window. Number each window.

GO

Follow the brief directions and pictured examples of one of the Advent calendars on this page. Hang it in a prominent place in your home and open one part each day, beginning December 1, OR give the calendar as a gift to someone special.

A SIMPLE CHRISTMAS TREE

GET READY
heavy, green construction paper
scissors
crayons
stickers — metallic stars and
  colored dots (optional)
cotton balls (optional)

GET SET
1. Trace the tree pattern on this page, and cut two of these shapes together from green construction paper.
2. Decorate both sides of both tree shapes with your crayons or stickers.
3. Cut a slot down the center of each tree shape, halfway along its length. Start at the bottom on one tree; start at the top on the other.

GO
Slide the two slots to fit together, and make your tree stand up!

CHRISTMAS TERRARIUM

YOU CAN PAINT FANCY THINGS ON THE LID

GET READY
a large jar or glass bowl with a lid
enough gravel to cover the bottom of
the container (an inch deep)
broken pieces of charcoal
potting soil
small plants (wild plants OR house
plants)
sprigs of holly, mistletoe, or
evergreen
artificial red berries
a red bow

GET SET
1. Mix gravel and charcoal and place in the bottom of a large jar or glass bowl.
2. Add some soil, mixed with a little more charcoal. Make a little well in the soil for each plant. Set the plants gently in the wells.
3. Add holly, mistletoe, or evergreen sprigs in and around the plants. Add artificial berries for color.
4.
5. Add just enough water to dampen the soil, and cover the jar.

GO
Tie a huge red ribbon around the jar and give your terrarium to someone special. Don't forget to make a pretty tag or card.

BARBECUE CHARCOAL

POTTING SOIL

GRAVEL

the CREATION CONNECTION

Christmas

One reason the Lord made man was to tend and care for His creation. In many places around the world Christmas customs include gifts to the animals. This one is for the birds!

GET READY

a small, living tree or bush
string
heavy needle and thread
scissors, kitchen knife
cookie cutters
peanut butter, suet, nuts, diced fruits, bread, fat
 drippings, popcorn, cranberries
nylon netting (from vegetable and fruit bags)

GET SET

Choose a small, living tree or bush near a window
 where you can enjoy watching the birds.

GO

Decorate the tree with good things for birds to eat.
Seeds and fat are the best diet to help birds have
good energy and keep warm. Here are some ideas for
preparing a birds' feast for your tree.

- Cut oranges in half and scoop out the rind. Fill it with seeds and nuts and hang it like a small basket on the tree.
- Stuff a pine cone with hardened fat drippings or peanut butter and hang the cone from the tree.
- String popcorn, apple pieces, and cranberries together to make delicious ropes for the tree.
- Cut squares, triangles, or star shapes of suet. String with needle and thread to hang on the tree.
- Cut bread into fancy shapes with cookie cutters Spread each shape with butter, peanut butter, or softened fat which will harden when hung outside. String with needle and thread to hang on the tree.
- Mix seeds with fat and bread crumbs, and spoon mixture into pieces of nylon netting. Then tie corners together and hang from tree.

Watch as the birds in your neighborhood enjoy their
special gift.

A CHRISTMAS TREE FOR THE BIRDS

the CREATION CONNECTION

Taking care of God's Creation
Christmas

143

LOVING HANDS WREATH

GET READY
green construction paper
pencil
scissors
wide red ribbon (or large,
    ready-made bow)

GET SET
1. Draw around your hand.
2. Using your hand as a
    pattern, cut 20-30 green
    construction-paper hands.
3. Arrange the hands in a
    circle to form a wreath.
4. Glue each hand in place.
5. Add a large red bow.

GO
Hang your wreath in a place where it
will bring loveliness and joy to
someone else.

NOTE: *1) When used as a group project, each member of the group may
contribute two hands.
2) Use pastel colors to make a
"happy" wreath any time of year.*

the **CREATION CONNECTION**
Christmas gift for a sick
friend or elderly shut-in
Christmas decoration for
a room or door
Year-round
"happy" wreath

A CHRISTMAS CENTERPIECE

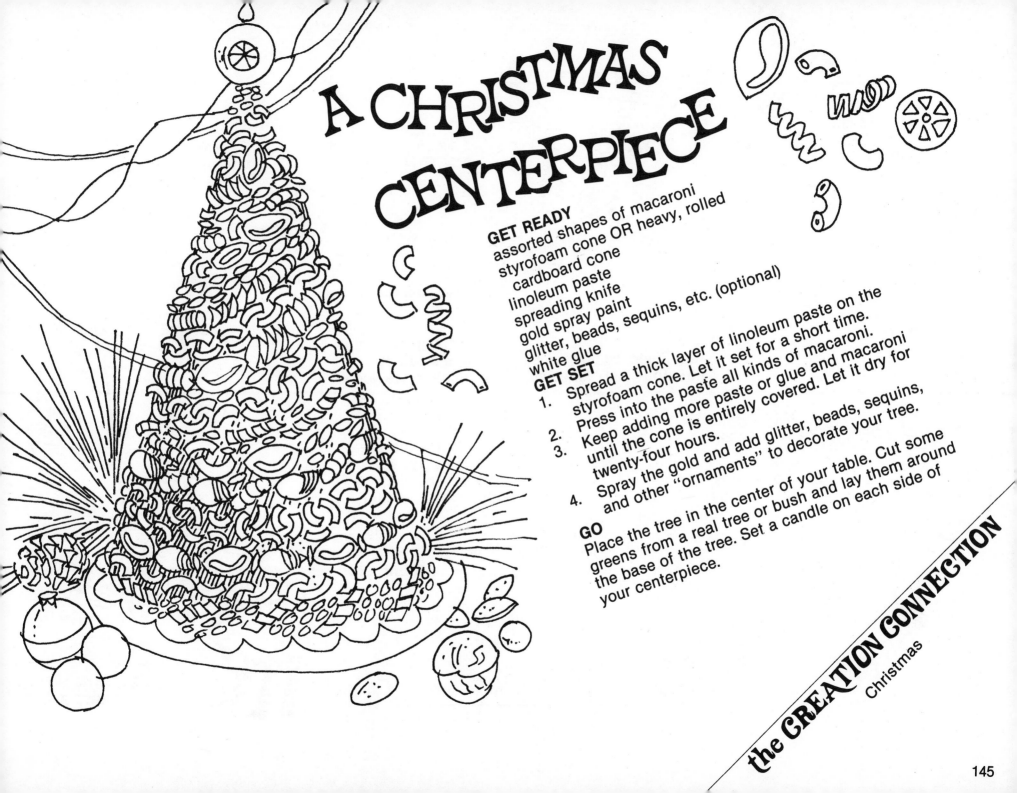

GET READY
assorted shapes of macaroni
styrofoam cone OR heavy, rolled
cardboard cone
linoleum paste
spreading knife
gold spray paint
glitter, beads, sequins, etc. (optional)
white glue

GET SET

1. Spread a thick layer of linoleum paste on the styrofoam cone. Let it set for a short time. Press into the paste all kinds of macaroni.

2. Keep adding more paste or glue and macaroni until the cone is entirely covered. Let it dry for twenty-four hours.

3. Spray the gold and add glitter, beads, sequins, and other "ornaments" to decorate your tree.

GO
Place the tree in the center of your table. Cut some greens from a real tree or bush and lay them around the base of the tree. Set a candle on each side of your centerpiece.

the CREATION CONNECTION

Christmas

145

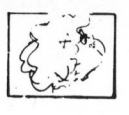

All Kinds of Angels

PIPE CLEANER FOR A HALO

YARN HAIR

STYROFOAM BALL FOR HEAD

ATTACH PAPER WINGS TO BACK WITH TAPE.

SIMPLE PAPER CONE FOR BODY

Cone angel

Felt or paper angel

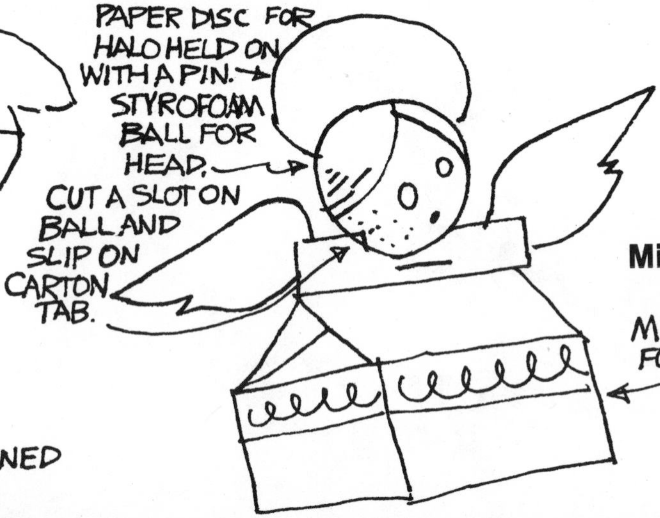

HALO IS A PAPER DISC PINNED INTO HEAD

YARN FOR HAIR

STYROFOAM BALL FOR HEAD

PAPER SONG BOOK WILL FASTEN ON WITH TWO DROPS OF GLUE

PLASTIC HAND CREAM OR SOAP BOTTLE

Bottle angel

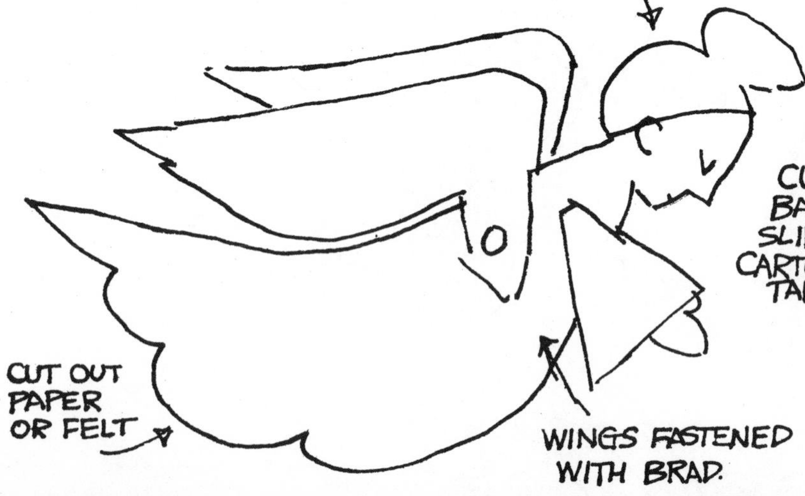

GET READY
cardboards, metallic papers, construction
  paper
glue
scraps of metallic trims and braids,
  beads, sequins, etc.
stapler, felt scraps
brass paper fastener
a pop bottle
a half-pint milk carton

GET SET
Look at the pictures on this page. They show you how to make different kinds of angels, using the materials listed above.

GO
Follow the directions in the pictures to make your favorite kind of angel.

CUT OUT PAPER OR FELT

WINGS FASTENED WITH BRAD.

PAPER DISC FOR HALO HELD ON WITH A PIN.

STYROFOAM BALL FOR HEAD.

CUT A SLOT ON BALL AND SLIP ON CARTON TAB.

Milk carton angel

MILK CARTON FOR BODY

the CREATION CONNECTION

Christmas

SWEDISH PEACE TREE

In Sweden, boys and girls sometimes make "trees" like the one on this page to symbolize peace on earth. We know that real peace is only possible through Jesus Christ. The star on the top of the tree represents the Star of the East and reminds us of His birth in Bethlehem.

GET READY

wood lattice strips
glue or wood stapler
a flower pot or pail
sand, water
eight small, red apples
red ribbon or yarn
ornaments or cut-out cookies

GET SET

1. Cut lattice so that you have one long support stick and four "branches"—each one slightly shorter than the last.
2. Secure the "branches" in place by stapling or gluing ... OR tie them in place with red ribbon or yarn.
3. Fill pot or pail with sand and pour water in to make it damp. (Decorate the pot if you wish.) Insert the "tree" firmly in the sand.
4. Stick an apple into each end of the cross branches. Hang cookies or ornaments from the branches.
5. Be sure to place a star on top.

How 'bout a PASTRY PARTRIDGE in a PEACE TREE?

the CREATION CONNECTION

Christmas ... peace on earth.

147

CRÈCHE FIGURES

Cone Figures
1. Cut half-circle—six to eight inches for adults, smaller for children.
2. Cut a tiny half-circle where a styrofoam or rolled-paper ball will sit for a head.
3. Make capes of slightly smaller half-circles.
4. Put together with white glue.

Paper Tube Figures
1. Use paper tubes as bodies; Ping-Pong balls or styrofoam balls for heads.
2. Wrap balls in white tissue paper and stuff tissue down into tube to hold on head.
3. Then draw on facial features.
4. Make clothing of felt or colored paper. Trim with cloth scraps, yarn and braid.

STYROFOAM BALL

MAKE A PAPER CONE

WRAP THIS AROUND

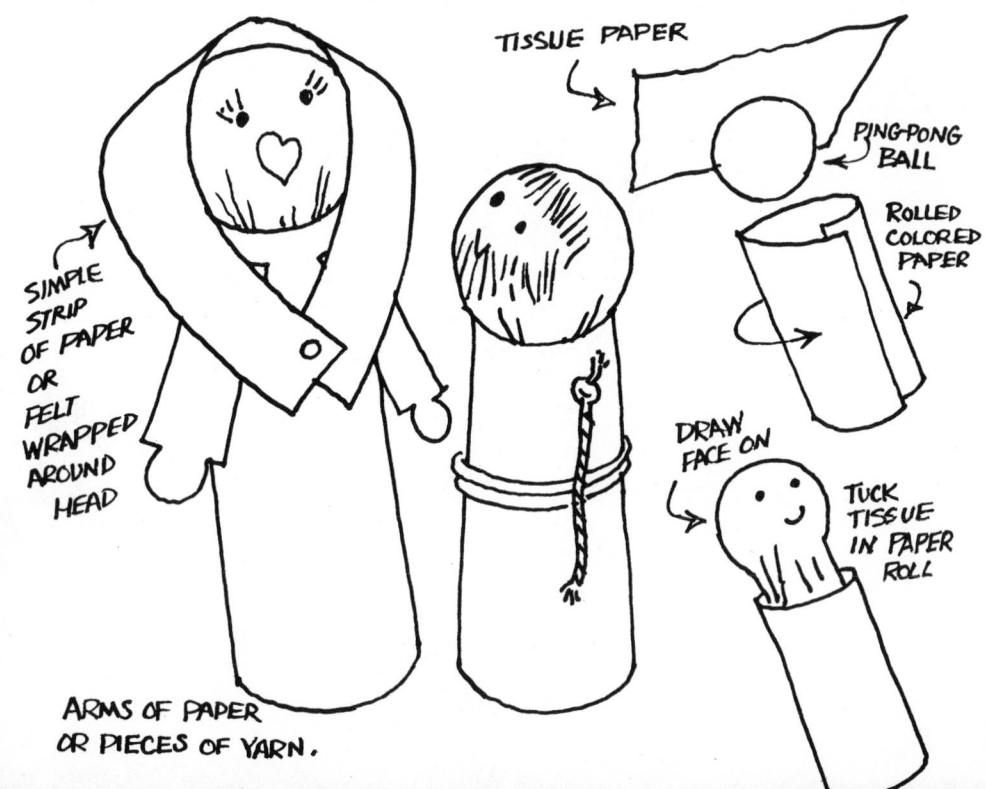

SIMPLE STRIP OF PAPER OR FELT WRAPPED AROUND HEAD

TISSUE PAPER

PING-PONG BALL

ROLLED COLORED PAPER

DRAW FACE ON

TUCK TISSUE IN PAPER ROLL

ARMS OF PAPER OR PIECES OF YARN.

Clay Figures

1. Shape figures from modeling clay or use the play clay recipe in this book.
2. Paint with tempera or acrylic paints.
3. Use braids and trims, cloth scraps and yarns for added features.

MAKE A "WORM" OF CLAY & WRAP AROUND HEAD

BEARDS ARE FUN TO MAKE. JUST MAKE A LOT OF "WORMS" & STICK THEM ON.

A BALL OF CLAY

A "HOT DOG" OF CLAY

A "LOG" OF CLAY

NOW PUT THEM ALL TOGETHER

"HOT DOG" OF CLAY FOR FIGURE

A PRESSED OUT "BLANKET" OF CLAY

NOW PUT THE "BLANKET" AROUND THE "HOT DOG"

Bread-Dough Figures

You Need:
24 white bread slices (cut off crusts)
white glue
Vaseline
white glue and water (mixed in equal parts)
food coloring
(This recipe will make 6 to 8 three-inch figures.)

Crumble bread into a bowl. Add 12 ounces of white glue. Rub vaseline on your hands and knead the mixture until it is no longer sticky. Divide the mixture into as many parts as you want colors to work with. Add food coloring to each part and knead in color. Make the basic body shapes of uncolored dough. Then use the water and glue mixture to attach decorative, colored features and clothing. Press the details onto each figure firmly, then brush the entire figure with the glue and water mixture.

PIECE OF CLOTH AROUND HEAD WITH A RUBBER BAND

FOR SHEEP: MAKE SAUSAGE SHAPE & COVER WITH LITTLE DOUGH BALLS.

PAPER CLIP STRAIGHTENED INTO STAFF

MAKE FIGURE OUT OF DOUGH JUST LIKE CLAY FIGURES.

the CREATION CONNECTION

Christmas

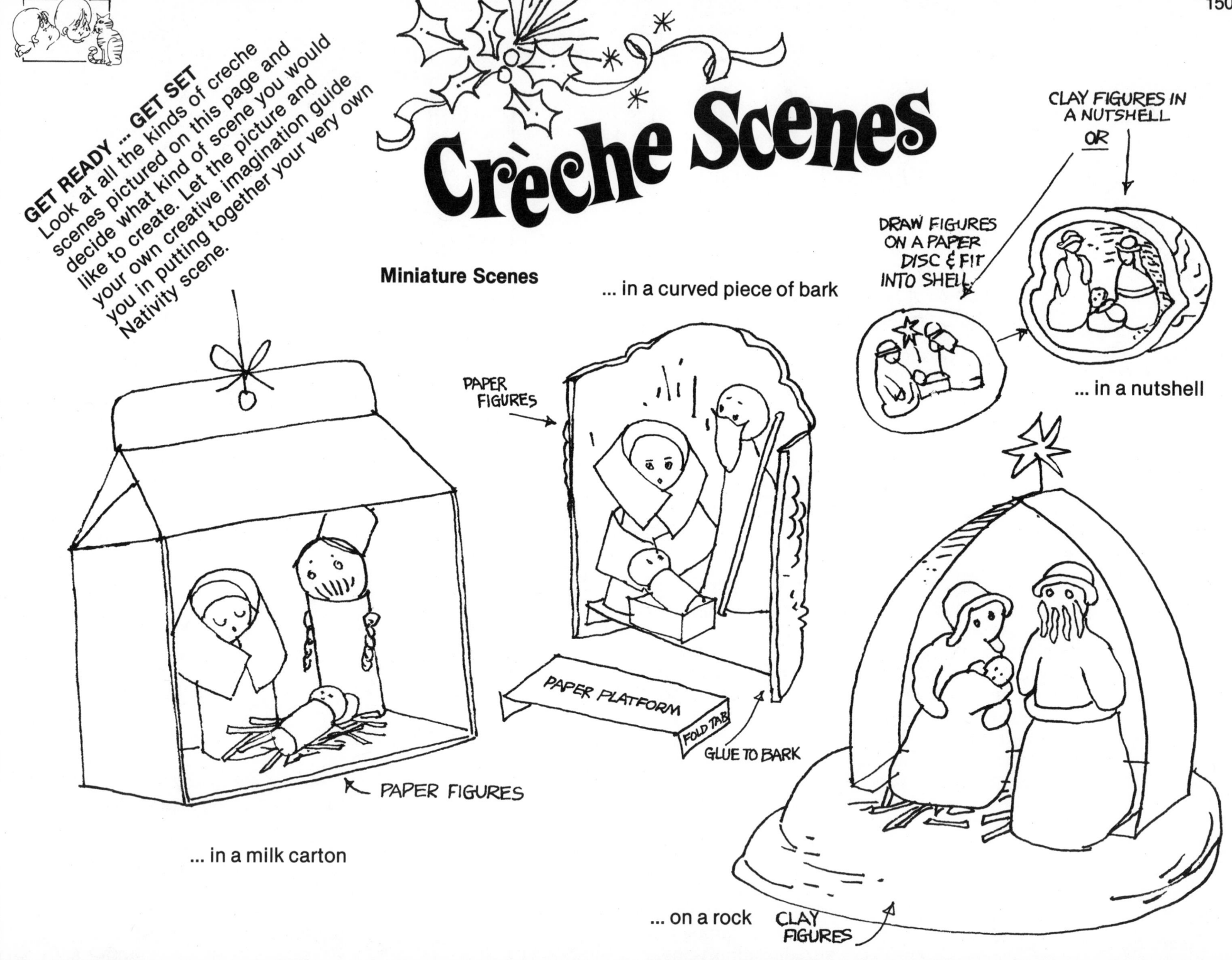

Crèche Scenes

Miniature Scenes

... in a curved piece of bark

CLAY FIGURES IN A NUTSHELL
OR

DRAW FIGURES ON A PAPER DISC & FIT INTO SHELL

... in a nutshell

PAPER FIGURES

PAPER PLATFORM

FOLD TAB

GLUE TO BARK

PAPER FIGURES

... in a milk carton

... on a rock   CLAY FIGURES

BARK

PIECE OF CLOTH

... in a cave setting made of stones, moss, bark, with dressed, dollhouse-size figures.

Larger Scenes

... in a tissue box or shoebox

KLEENEX OR SHOE BOX

HAT: PAPER RING

BEARD: COTTON BALL

ICE CREAM STICKS

... in a manger lean-to made of Popsicle sticks or tongue depressors, using sawed-off clothespins as base figures for people.

PAPER

HEAD! PING PONG BALL

PAPER ARMS ATTACH TO BOTH SIDES OF CONE.

GO
Place your finished Nativity scene in your room or somewhere where it can become a reminder to you and your family and friends to set aside a special time of worship each day during the Nativity season.

the CREATION CONNECTION
Christmas

151

Doorknob Decorations

REAL DOORKNOB

WREATH

ANGEL

STAR

GET READY
colored felt pieces and scraps
scissors
white glue OR needle and thread

GET SET
1. Use the pattern on the next page to cut a basic background shape for your doorknob decoration.
2. Look at the pictures to get ideas for add-on parts that will make an angel, wreath, candle, tree, or Christmas-related decorations.

GO
Make doorknob decorations for gifts or for all the doorknobs in your house. Each time you touch a doorknob, let the decoration remind you of the real meaning of Christmas.

the CREATION CONNECTION

Christmas

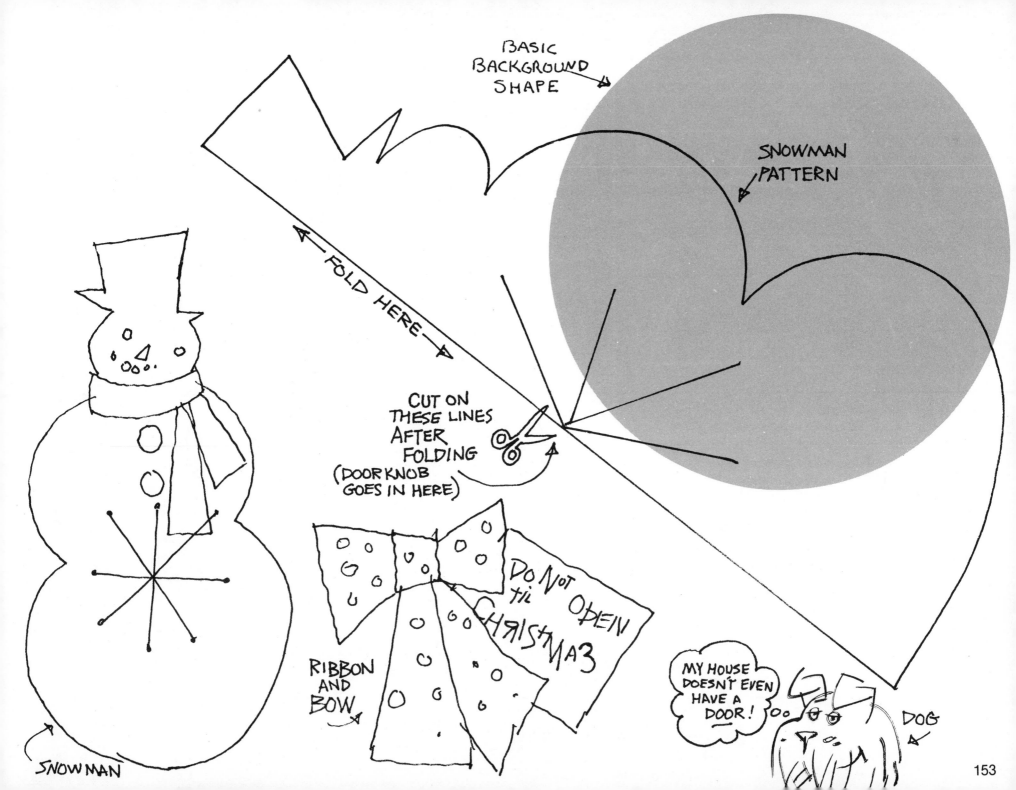

153

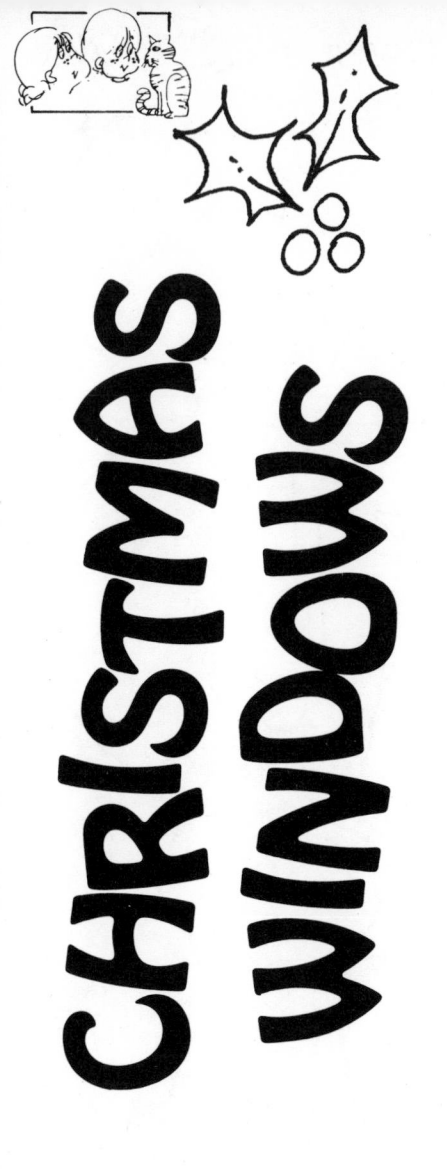

CHRISTMAS WINDOWS

SHEPHERD & ANGEL

GET READY
stiff paper OR tagboard
colored tissue paper OR any
    transparent material
scissors
pencil
clear glue

GET SET
1. Use the patterns on this page as basic shapes for planning and creating a nativity window scene.
2. Trace the shapes you need onto stiff paper or tagboard and cut them out. Use these as patterns to cut as many shapes as you need from different bright colors of tissue paper or acetate.

GO
Use clear glue to place shapes on glass windows or doors.

THAT'S REAL PURTY!

the CREATION CONNECTION

Christmas

MARY & JOSEPH

THREE WISE KINGS

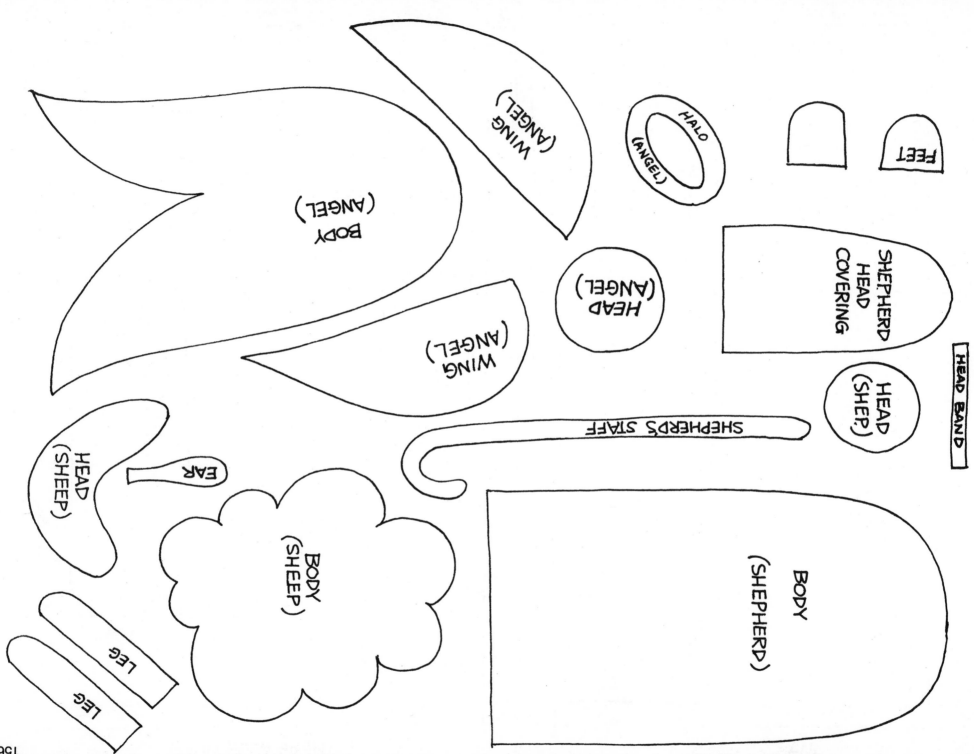

WING (ANGEL)

HALO (ANGEL)

FEET

BODY (ANGEL)

SHEPHERD HEAD COVERING

HEAD (ANGEL)

WING (ANGEL)

HEAD (SHEP.)

HEAD BAND

SHEPHERD'S STAFF

HEAD (SHEEP)

EAR

BODY (SHEEP)

BODY (SHEPHERD)

LEG

LEG

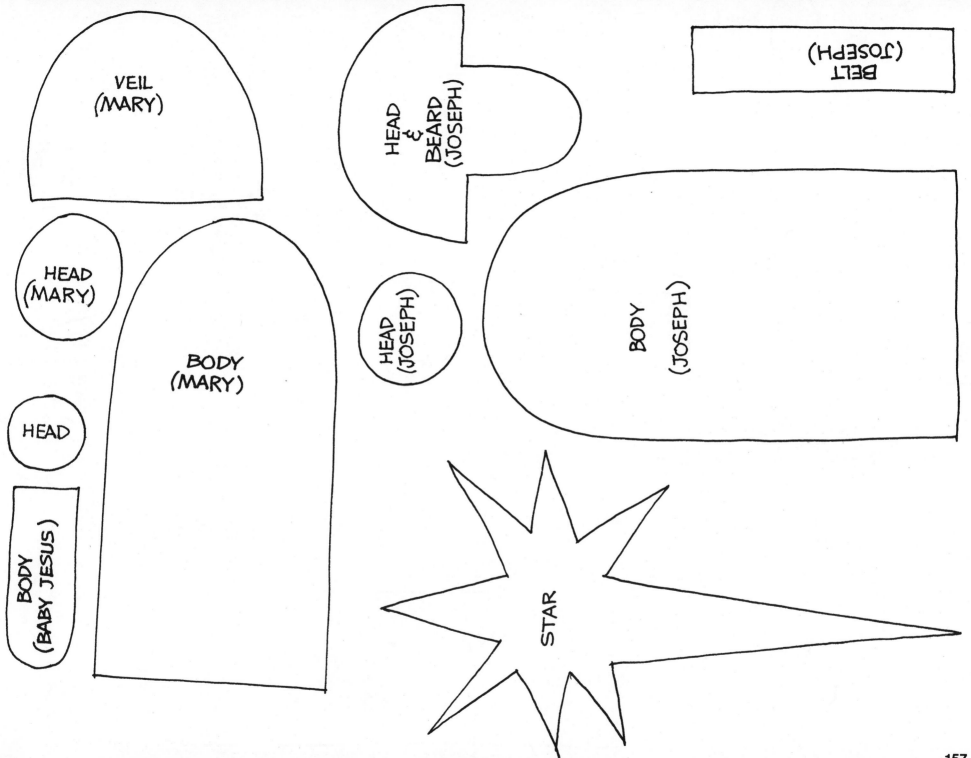

VEIL (MARY)

HEAD & BEARD (JOSEPH)

BELT (JOSEPH)

HEAD (MARY)

BODY (MARY)

HEAD (JOSEPH)

BODY (JOSEPH)

HEAD

BODY (BABY JESUS)

STAR

157

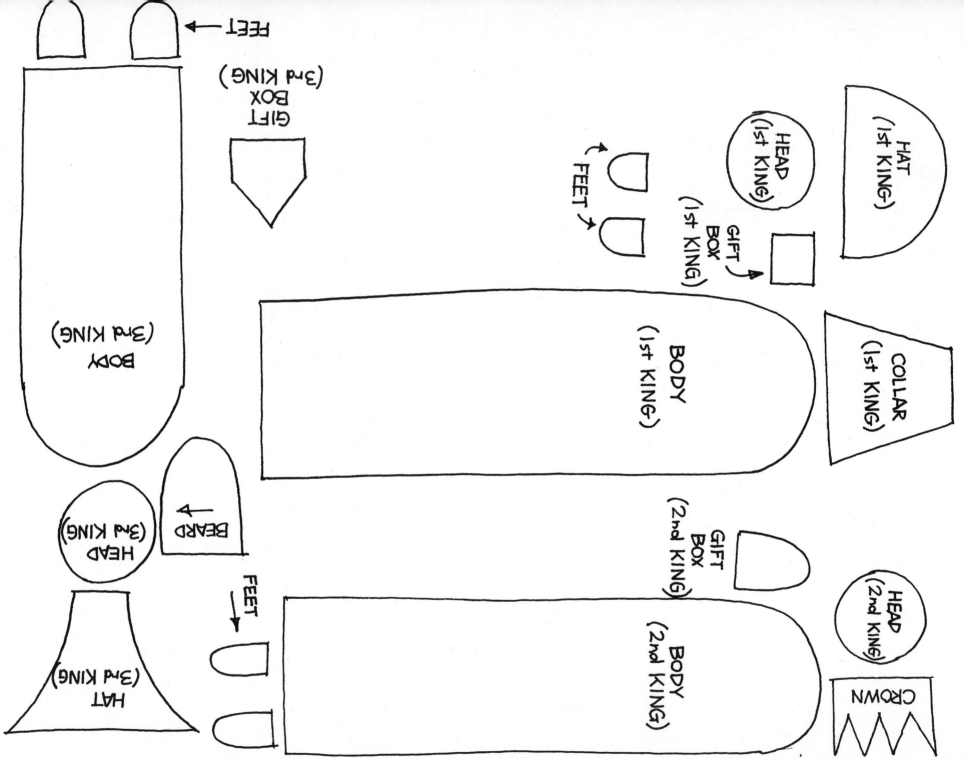

FEET

GIFT BOX (3rd KING)

HAT (1st KING)

HEAD (1st KING)

FEET

GIFT BOX (1st KING)

BODY (3rd KING)

BODY (1st KING)

COLLAR (1st KING)

HEAD (3rd KING)

BEARD

GIFT BOX (2nd KING)

HAT (3rd KING)

FEET

BODY (2nd KING)

HEAD (2nd KING)

CROWN

SCRIPTURE MEMORY

LINK A LOOP

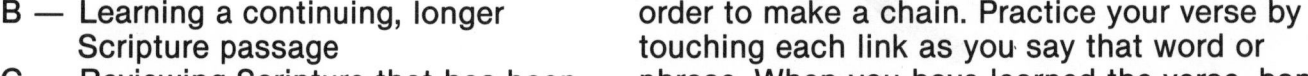

YOU NEED:
colored construction paper
felt-tip pen
scissors
paste

PURPOSE:
A — Practicing a single Scripture memory verse
B — Learning a continuing, longer Scripture passage
C — Reviewing Scripture that has been memorized over a long period of time

PURPOSE A:
Write each word or phrase of a memory verse on a colored paper strip. Link strips together in order to make a chain. Practice your verse by touching each link as you say that word or phrase. When you have learned the verse, hang your chain somewhere as a memory jogger for review.

PURPOSE B:
Put a separate verse of a long passage of Scripture on each link. Use it in the above manner to review the passage from time to time.

WHERE DOES THIS CHAIN LEAD?

IT LEADS TO LOTS OF FUN AND SPIRITUAL BLESSING!

THE LORD IS MY SHEPHERD I SHALL NOT WANT...

PURPOSE C:
Keep a chain of memory work, adding a link each time you learn a new verse. See how long you can make your chain. Use it frequently as a memory jogger to review all the verses. (Set a goal — like five or fifteen or fifty yards for the length of your chain. Then you can say, "Hey, I know fifty yards of Scripture!")

PURPOSE: Learning and reviewing single memory verses

YOU NEED:
hands, feet, fingers
washable felt-tip pens

Write the words and phrases of the verses you want to learn on your fingers, hands, feet with washable felt-tip pens. Ask your friends to help you practice saying the verses by lining up feet and hands in the right order.

Try hiding every other foot or hand and saying the verses with only half of the words showing. Repeat the verses over and over until you know them well.

NOTE: *Products like Fantastik, Mr. Clean, and 409 take off stubborn felt-tip pen marks in a hurry!*

SCRIPTURE MEMORY

FINGERS, HANDS 'N FEET

HANDY MEMORIZING AT YOUR FINGER TIPS

SCRIPTURE MEMORY

GOIN' FISHIN'

SCRIPTURE WORMS

PURPOSE:
A — Practicing matching Scripture verses with their references
B — A team contest for the same purpose
YOU NEED:
small strips of paper
a pencil
a can with a top
Bible
PURPOSE A:
Use your Bible to copy carefully the text of each of ten Scripture verses you have learned on separate strips of paper. Write each of the references for these verses on ten other strips of paper. Make a list of the verses and their references together on a large sheet of paper for an answer key. Fold and tape the key to the inside top of the can.

Curl all twenty strips of paper by winding them tightly around a pencil. Put your twenty "curly worms" in the can, put the top on and shake it. Now remove one worm from the can. Read what it says. If it is the text of a verse, give its reference. If it is a reference, say the corresponding verse. (Use the answer key to check yourself.) Continue until you have used all your worms. Then replace all the worms in the can and try over and over again until you get them all right.
PURPOSE B:
Divide a group of friends into two teams. Take turns "goin' fishin' " by choosing worms from the can. Each correct match is worth five points. The team with the most points wins.

NO GOOD FOR FISH BUT JUST THE THING FOR CATCHIN' PEOPLES!

A LINE AT A TIME

Cards on clothesline: BEHOLD I STAND / AT THE / DOOR AND KNOCK / IF / ANY MAN HEAR MY VOICE / AND OPEN THE DOOR / I WILL / COME INTO HIM

LET'S SEE NOW... WHICH CARD COMES NEXT?

AND HE / WITH ME / AND SUP WITH HIM / REV. 3:20

PURPOSE:

A—Learning or reviewing a single memory verse

B—A memory jogger for your room

C—A team relay

YOU NEED:

clothesline
clip-on clothespins
cards OR construction paper
felt-tip pen
Bible

PURPOSE A:

Write each word or phrase of the verse you want to learn on a separate card. Mix up the pile of cards so that they are out of order. Then pin them with clothespins on the line IN ORDER so that the verse reads from left to right. Take them down, mix them up, and try over and over again until you can say the verse without looking.

PURPOSE B:

Tie a line up in your room and "hang" a new memory verse every week.

PURPOSE C:

Hang two lines and make two card piles for each verse. Divide a group of friends into two relay teams. At the GO signal, the first member of each team "hangs" the verse. The second member takes it down, the third hangs it, etc. As the verse is hung, the rest of the team chants each word aloud. The team that finishes first wins.

BE / YE / KIND / ONE / TO / A...

YOU CAN HANG IT FROM YOUR BED POST LIKE THIS.

163

SCRIPTURE MEMORY

Let's play POST OFFICE

PURPOSE:

Reviewing Scripture memory work and/or matching verses with their references

YOU NEED:

brown construction paper
envelopes
3"X 5"cards
pen and pencil
scissors
paste
tape, pins (optional)

Make mailboxes out of envelopes by drawing "ends" and labeling the "front" of the box U.S. Mail.

Cut brown paper "posts" on which to mount your boxes. Paste the post to each box and tape or pin the boxes on the wall or bulletin board— OR lay them flat on a large table or floor space.

Write each Scripture verse you have learned on a 3"X 5"card. DO NOT include the reference. Write the reference as an address on the side of one of the mailboxes. Mix up the cards.

Now see if you can be a very efficient mail carrier and deliver each card to the right address. (To check yourself, look up each Scripture reference in your Bible.)

POP GOES THE WINNER!

SCRIPTURE MEMORY

PSALM 150 VERSE ONE!

"PRAISE GOD IN HIS SANCTUARY; PRAISE HIM IN HIS MIGHTY HEAVENS!"

COME ON MARY KAY! YOU CAN DO IT!

PURPOSE: A—Learning single Scripture verses

B—A team game for reviewing Scripture memory work

YOU NEED: balloons
permanent felt-tip pens
Bible
tape
large safety pins

REWARD POP

Write the words or phrases of a verse you want to learn on balloons. Pin or tape the balloons in order on a curtain or wall. Say the verse over and over. When you are sure you know the verse, letter perfect, reward yourself by popping each word as you say it!

RELAY POP

Put up ten plain balloons for each team. Divide people into two teams. Call out a Scripture reference to one team. If the first player on a team can say the verse perfectly, he gets to pop one of his team's balloons. If not, the opposing team gets a chance. The team with the fewest balloons left at the end wins.

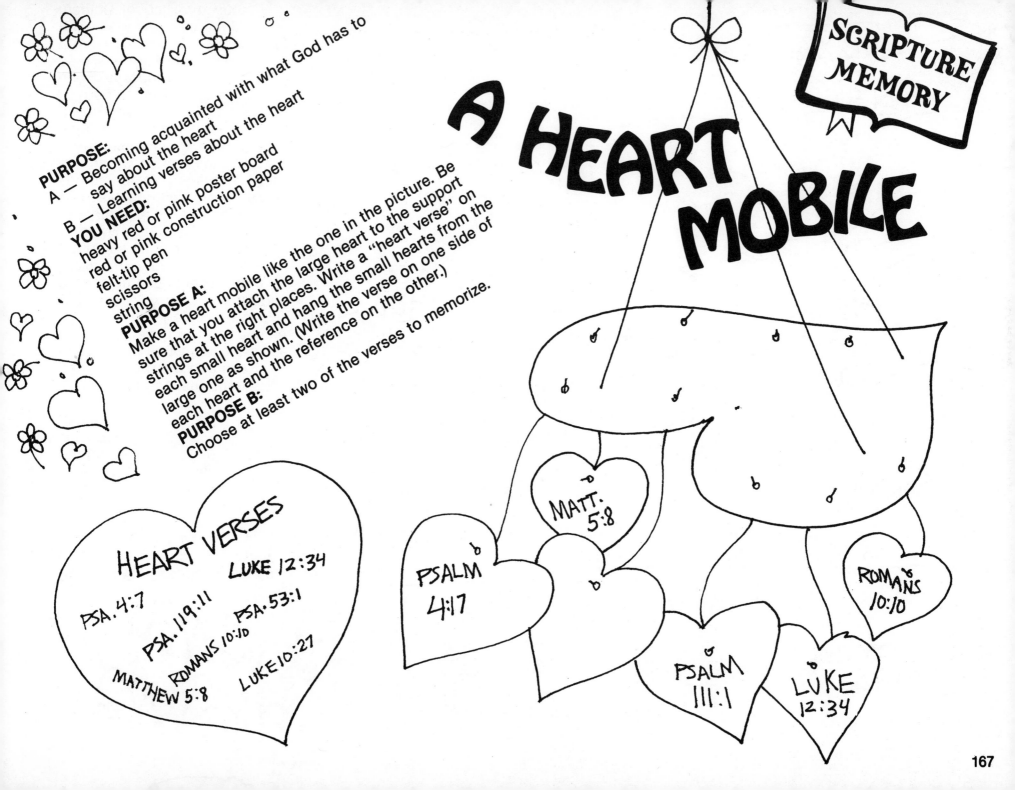

A HEART MOBILE

PURPOSE:
A — Becoming acquainted with what God has to say about the heart
B — Learning verses about the heart

YOU NEED:
heavy red or pink poster board
red or pink construction paper
felt-tip pen
scissors
string

PURPOSE A:
Make a heart mobile like the one in the picture. Be sure that you attach the large heart to the support strings at the right places. Write a "heart verse" on each small heart and hang the small hearts from the large one as shown. (Write the verse on one side of each heart and the reference on the other.)

PURPOSE B:
Choose at least two of the verses to memorize.

HEART VERSES
LUKE 12:34
PSA. 4:7
PSA. 119:11   PSA. 53:1
ROMANS 10:10
MATTHEW 5:8   LUKE 10:27

PSALM 4:17
MATT. 5:8
PSALM 111:1
LUKE 12:34
ROMANS 10:10

167

TWINKLE TWINKLE

SCRIPTURE MEMORY

PURPOSE: Practicing single Scripture memory verses

YOU NEED:
yellow, green, and brown construction paper
felt-tip pen
scissors
paste

Use green construction paper to create a tree like one on this page. Make a piece of tree for each word or phrase of your verse. Beginning with the treetop, write one word or phrase on each piece. Cut a brown trunk and write the reference on it. Practice the verse by laying the parts together like a tree puzzle as you say each part aloud. When you can quote the entire verse without looking at your tree, reward yourself by cutting a gold star and placing it on top of the tree.

Then paste your tree, trunk, and star together permanently by overlapping the edges of the parts just slightly and hang it where it will be a good memory jogger for review.

TRUST IN THE LORD

WITH ALL THINE HEART;

AND LEAN NOT UNTO THINE OWN UNDERSTANDING.

IN ALL THY WAYS ACKNOWLEDGE HIM,

AND HE SHALL DIRECT THY PATHS.

PROVERBS 3:5-6

THE WORD OF OUR GOD SHALL STAND FOREVER.
ISAIAH 40:8

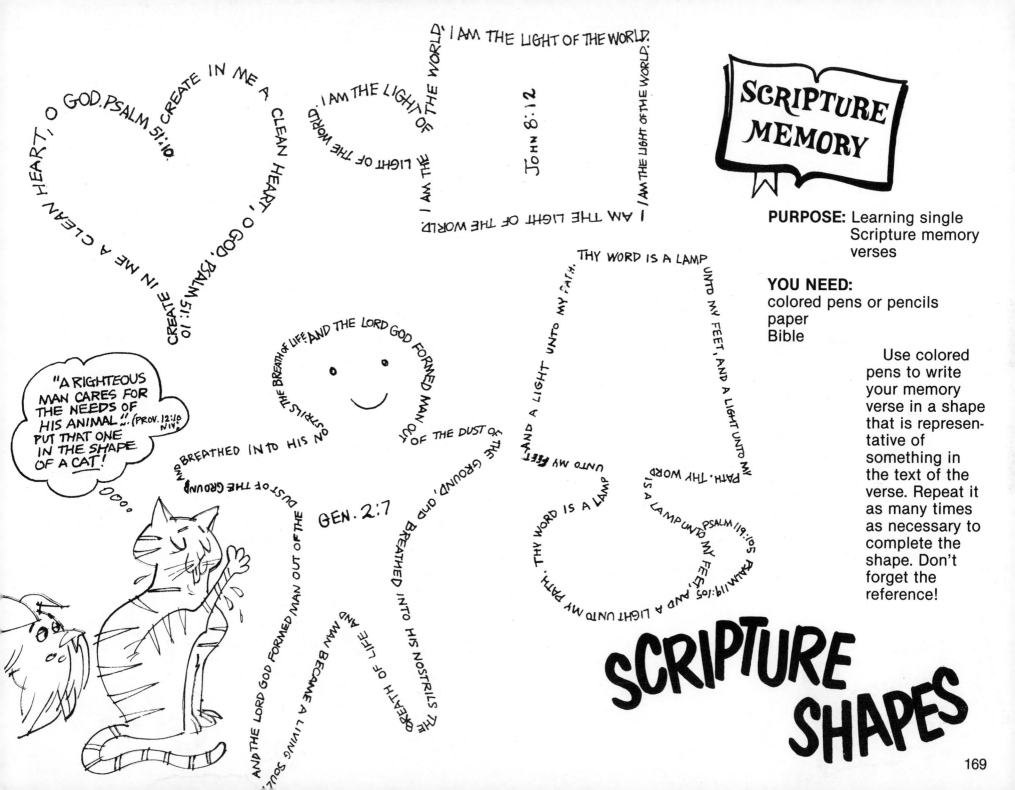

CREATE IN ME A CLEAN HEART, O GOD. PSALM 51:10

I AM THE LIGHT OF THE WORLD. JOHN 8:12

SCRIPTURE MEMORY

PURPOSE: Learning single Scripture memory verses

YOU NEED:
colored pens or pencils
paper
Bible

Use colored pens to write your memory verse in a shape that is representative of something in the text of the verse. Repeat it as many times as necessary to complete the shape. Don't forget the reference!

"A RIGHTEOUS MAN CARES FOR THE NEEDS OF HIS ANIMAL." (PROV. 12:10 NIV). PUT THAT ONE IN THE SHAPE OF A CAT!

AND THE LORD GOD FORMED MAN OUT OF THE DUST OF THE GROUND, AND BREATHED INTO HIS NOSTRILS THE BREATH OF LIFE AND MAN BECAME A LIVING SOUL. GEN. 2:7

THY WORD IS A LAMP UNTO MY FEET, AND A LIGHT UNTO MY PATH. PSALM 119:105

SCRIPTURE SHAPES

HAND IN HAND

SCRIPTURE MEMORY

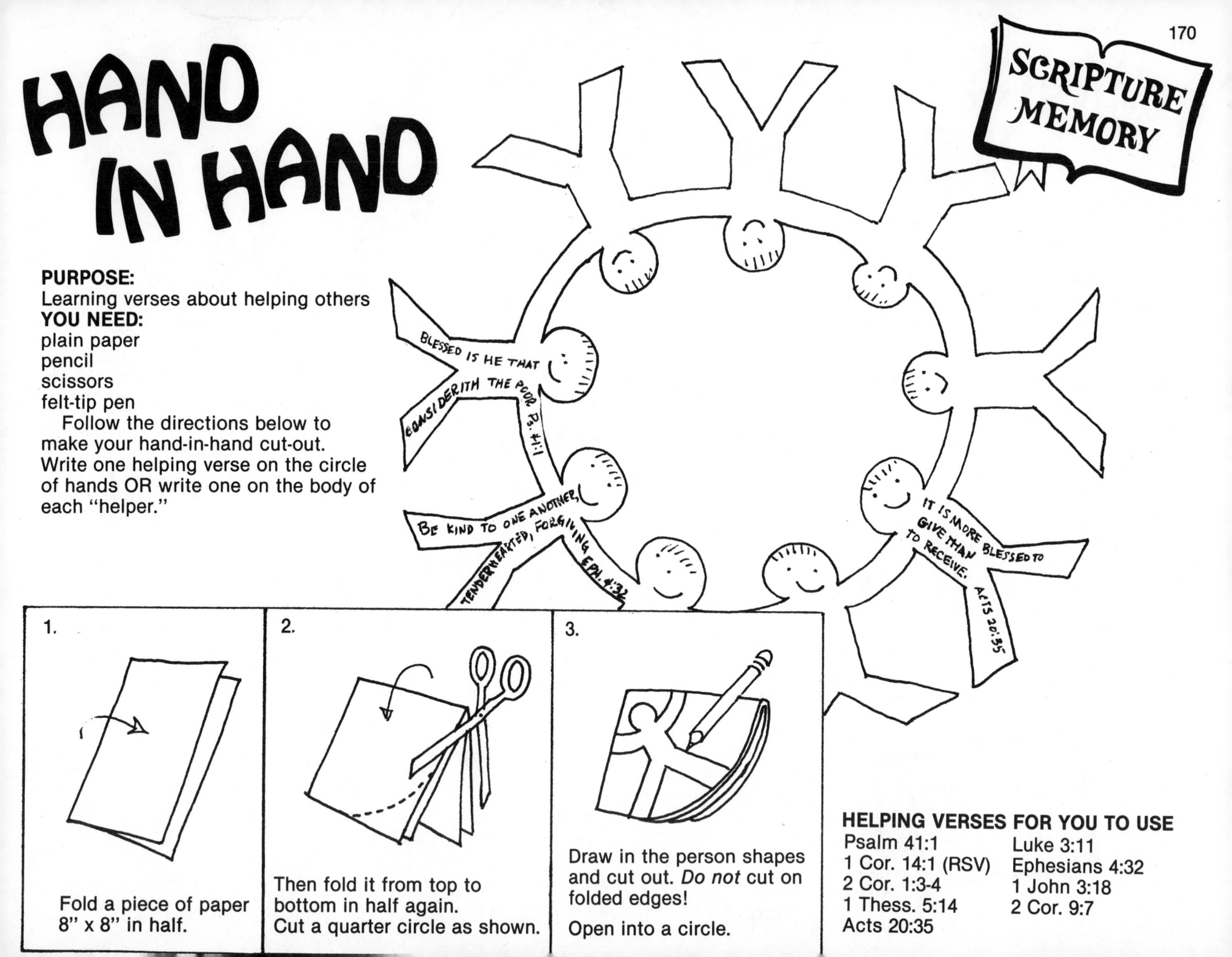

PURPOSE:
Learning verses about helping others
YOU NEED:
plain paper
pencil
scissors
felt-tip pen
  Follow the directions below to make your hand-in-hand cut-out. Write one helping verse on the circle of hands OR write one on the body of each "helper."

BLESSED IS HE THAT CONSIDERITH THE POOR Ps. 41:1

BE KIND TO ONE ANOTHER, TENDERHEARTED, FORGIVING EPH. 4:32

IT IS MORE BLESSED TO GIVE THAN TO RECEIVE. ACTS 20:35

1.
Fold a piece of paper 8" x 8" in half.

2.
Then fold it from top to bottom in half again.
Cut a quarter circle as shown.

3.
Draw in the person shapes and cut out. *Do not* cut on folded edges!

Open into a circle.

HELPING VERSES FOR YOU TO USE

Psalm 41:1	Luke 3:11
1 Cor. 14:1 (RSV)	Ephesians 4:32
2 Cor. 1:3-4	1 John 3:18
1 Thess. 5:14	2 Cor. 9:7
Acts 20:35	

SCRIPTURE MEMORY

Memorize 'n Munch!

PURPOSE:

Learning or reviewing Scripture verses while you eat!!

YOU NEED:
clear, envelope-type place mats OR clear contact paper
12 X 18 construction paper
crayons & felt-tip pens
Bible

Use construction paper, crayons, and pens to make a place mat on which is written a Bible verse you would like to learn or review. Decorate your mat to make it attractive. Cover with clear contact paper OR slip into a clear, envelope-type place mat cover. Use the mat each time you eat a meal until you learn the verse. Then make a new mat to help you learn another verse. Make a mat for each member of the family. When each person has learned his verse, trade mats!

SCRIPTURE MEMORY

SCRIPTURE SECRETS

PURPOSE: Learning and reviewing memory verses Here are some ideas for writing your Scripture verses in a way that no one else can decipher immediately. Try one or more of them for fun.

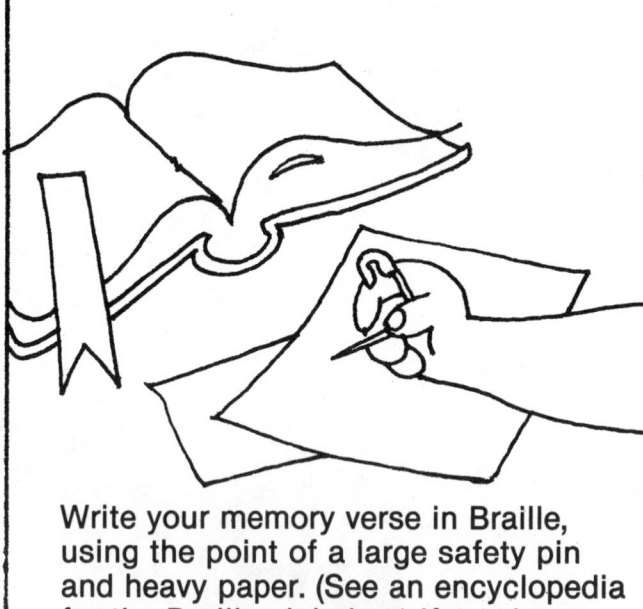

Write them in code. Then make a code key and see if a friend can "break" the code and translate the words and references perfectly.

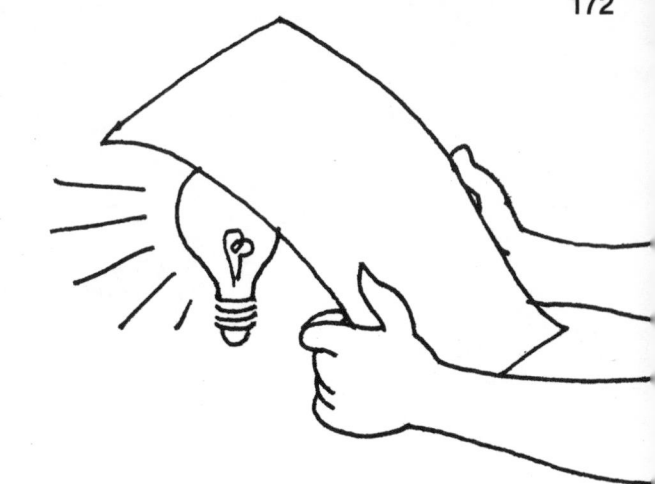

Use a Q-tip and lemon juice OR evaporated milk to write your verse. Make it reappear by warming the paper over an electric light bulb or radiator. (Don't get too close!)

Write your memory verse in Braille, using the point of a large safety pin and heavy paper. (See an encyclopedia for the Braille alphabet.) If you have a friend who reads Braille, try it out on him!

Place some waxed paper over your paper. Press VERY hard as you write your memory verse. Give a friend the "plain" piece of paper and tell him to brush it with a light, thin "wash" of paint, then read the message back to you.

DAISIES DO TELL

SCRIPTURE MEMORY

HERE'S HOW

HOW BEAUTIFUL UPON THE MOUNTAIN ARE THE FEET OF...

PURPOSE:
Reinforcing the Scripture memory concept

YOU NEED:
lots of field daisies (buttercups or dandelions may be substituted)
a head and heart full of Scripture
friends

Arrange the flowers in a big bouquet in the center of the floor or table. Take turns saying Scripture verses you have learned. For each verse a person can correctly say, he/she gets one daisy. Make a little slit with your fingernail near the bottom of each daisy stem. Slip another daisy stem through the slot and continue to make a long chain. When you have all had a wonderful time saying all the chains you can recall, complete your daisy chains by closing the circle to make a necklace or headband.

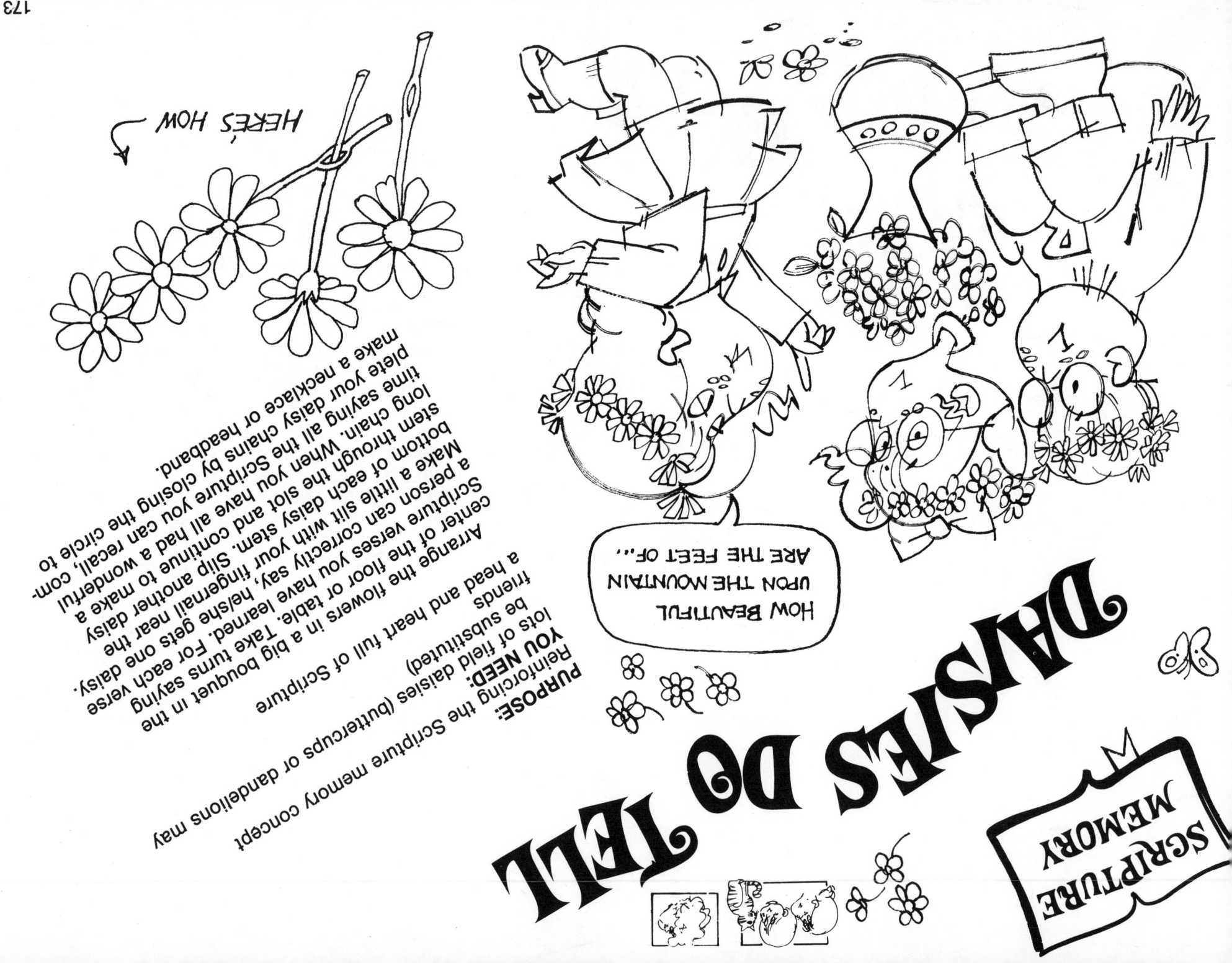

174

SCRIPTURE MEMORY

BODY TICK-TACK-TOE

PURPOSE:

A team game for reviewing Scripture memory work

YOU NEED:

chairs (optional)
chalk or masking tape
a list of Bible verses with references

Divide the people into two groups (X's & O's). Use the chalk or tape to make a tick-tack-toe grid on the floor. (Put a chair in each square if you wish.) Give a Scripture reference OR the first three words of a Scripture verse to the first member of the X team. If he can quote the verse, he places himself in any square he chooses. Repeat, alternating teams until one team gets three consecutive squares and wins. Play the game as long as everyone is having fun.

BERNY, CAN YOU SAY JOHN 1:10?

the Love Knot

PURPOSE: Learning a verse about love.

YOU NEED:
paper
pen or pencil
scissors
crayons (optional)

A FRIEND LOVETH AT ALL TIMES. A FRIEND LOVETH AT ALL TIMES. A FRIEND LOVETH AT ALL TIMES. A FRIEND LOVETH AT ALL TIMES.

LOOKS LIKE A BIG, BIG DOG BONE!

NOW I'M GETTIN' HUNGRY!

Trace this pattern. Cut it out carefully. Choose a verse about love. Write it in continuous fashion on both sides of the knot. Color it if you wish and hang it where it will be a constant reminder to you.

SCRIPTURE MEMORY

SCRIPTURE ABC's

MY SCRIPTURE BOOK

THE ALPHABET BOOK

PURPOSE:
Learning Scripture verses that begin with a given letter of the alphabet. (That's twenty-six verses ... in English!)

GET READY
colored construction paper
paper punch
yarn
crayons, felt-tip pens
scissors
Bible

Cut twenty-six pieces of bright, colored paper — all the same size. With crayons, write a large letter of the alphabet on each page. Then, find a short Scripture verse that begins with the letter A, one with B, and so on for all twenty-six letters. Carefully write the verse with its reference on each page. Use a paper punch to make holes, and string yarn through the holes to make a book of your twenty-six verses in ABC order! Learn them all so that you can "read" the book with your eyes shut!

ALL HAVE SINNED, AND COME SHORT OF THE GLORY OF GOD. ROM. 3:23

BE YE DOERS OF THE WORD, AND NOT HEARERS ONLY. JAMES 1:22

THE ALPHABET TREE

YOU NEED:
brown construction paper OR a real tree
    branch "planted" in a pot filled with sand
    or plaster
construction paper for making "fruit"
scissors
felt-tip pen
small basket

Make an alphabet tree similar to the one on this page. Use a real branch or paper. Cut twenty-six pieces of fruit from colored construction paper. Find a short verse for each letter of the alphabet. Write it on a piece of fruit and put it in the "fruit basket." Devour a piece of fruit each week by learning the verse and reference. Begin with the letter A. When you can say it perfectly, hang it on the tree. Continue until you have a whole harvest of fruit hanging on the tree. (Hint: Each time you review, say ALL the verses you have already learned.)

SCRIPTURE ABC's

"**A**ll have sinned, and come short of the glory of God" (Rom. 3:23).

"**B**elieve on the Lord Jesus Christ, and thou shalt be saved" (Acts 16:31).

"**C**reate in me a clean heart, O God" (Ps. 51:10).

"**D**o that which is honest" (2 Cor. 13:7).

"**E**very good gift and every perfect gift is from above" (James 1:17).

"**F**or the wages of sin is death; but the gift of God is eternal life through Jesus Christ our Lord" (Rom. 6:23).

"**G**od is our refuge and strength, a very present help in trouble" (Ps. 46:1).

"**H**onour thy father and thy mother" (Exod. 20:12).

"**I**t is a good thing to give thanks unto the Lord" (Ps. 92:1).

"**J**udge not, that ye be not judged" (Matt. 7:1).

"**K**now ye that the Lord he is God: it is he that hath made us, and not we ourselves" (Ps. 100:3).

"**L**ie not one to another" (Col. 3:9).

"**M**ake a joyful noise unto the Lord" (Ps. 100:1).

"**N**either is there salvation in any other: for there is none other name under heaven given among men, whereby we must be saved" (Acts 4:12).

"**O**bey them that have the rule over you" (Heb. 13:17).

"**P**ut on the whole armour of God, that ye may be able to stand against the wiles of the devil" (Eph. 6:11).

"**Q**uench not the Spirit" (1 Thess. 5:10).

"**R**emember the sabbath day, to keep it holy" (Exod. 20:8).

"**S**et your affection on things above, not on things on earth" (Col. 3:2).

"**T**hou shalt love the Lord thy God with all thy heart, and with all thy soul, and with all thy mind" (Matt. 22:37).

"**U**nto you is born this day in the city of David a Saviour, which is Christ the Lord" (Luke 2:11).

"**V**erily, verily, I say unto you, Whatsoever ye shall ask the Father in my name, he will give it you" (John 16:23).

"**W**hatsoever ye do in word or deed, do all in the name of the Lord Jesus, giving thanks to God and the Father by him" (Col. 3:17).

"e**X**cept a man be born again, he cannot see the kingdom of God" (John 3:3).

"**Y**e are the light of the world" (Matt. 5:14).

"Be **Z**ealous therefore, and repent" (Rev. 3:19).

BULLETIN BOARD

A Get-Acquainted Board

Each member of the group must cut the letters of his name from fabric, construction paper, or wallpaper, using his own free-style lettering. On the letters, he writes information about himself—single words and phrases that describe him—and draws representative pictures or cuts them from magazines to paste on the letters. He then arranges his name on the board for everyone to enjoy.

". . . May your roots go down deep into the soil of God's marvelous love . . ." (Eph. 3:17 LB). "Whatsoever a man soweth, that shall he also reap" (Gal. 6:7).

Growing in the LORD !

Look up each Scripture reference below. (You may want to add more references on your own!) Make a different flower for each verse you will use on your board. "Plant" each flower in your bulletin board garden, and read the verses each day to remind yourself of good ways to keep on growing in the Lord.

WHATCHA DOIN' ALIZABETH ?

I'M CULTIVATING A BEAUTIFUL SPIRIT !

Col. 2:7 LB
Phil. 3:12 LB
Rev. 1:3
Isa. 40:31
Col. 3:2
2 Peter 1:6 LB
2 Peter 1:8 LB

Jer. 33:3
Ps. 116:17
Lam. 3:25-26
Rom. 12:1
2 Peter 1:2 LB
2 Tim. 2:22

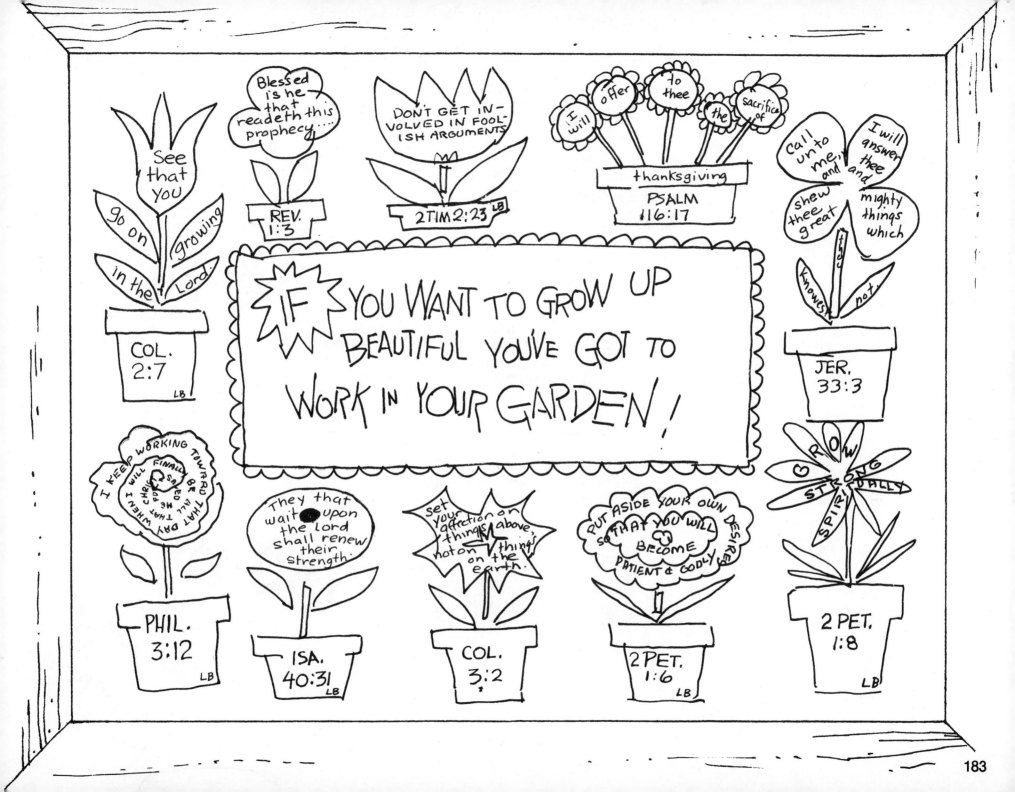

Bible Story Review

BULLETIN BOARD

JUST FOR FUN, YOU COULD MAKE THE BACKGROUND ON THIS ONE 3 DIFFERENT COLORS!

A Matching Game for Reviewing Familiar Bible Stories

Make a board just like the one on this page. (The shapes in the pattern section of this book will help you.) Try to match each name with one of the pictured objects by touching the object with one hand while touching the matching name with the other hand. As you touch each pair, tell the story it represents. Add some of your own matching pairs to the board, and try them out on your friends!

Jonah — fish
Peter — rooster
David — sling
Moses — baby basket
Noah — dove OR rainbow
Daniel — lion
Shadrach and Co. — fire
Boy — 5 loaves, 2 fishes
Rahab — rope
Joseph — striped coat
Balaam — donkey
Prodigal son — pigs
Samson — fox with tail on fire

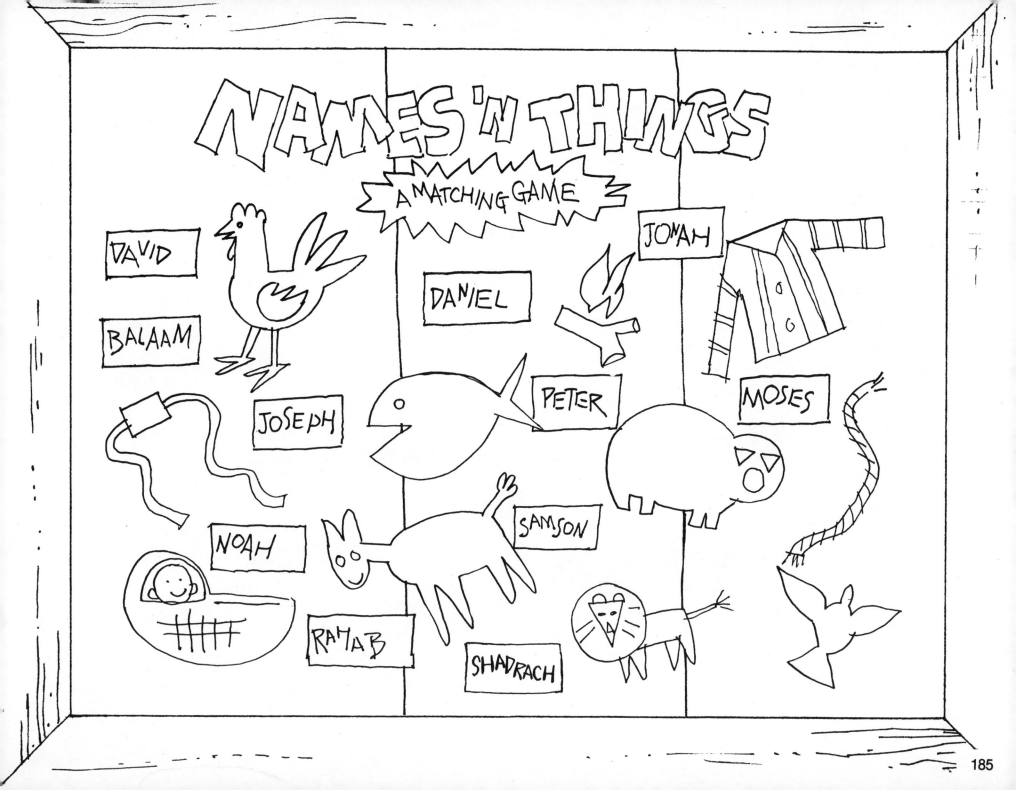

When the Bible Says, "Yes" or "No"

Use the STOP and GO patterns on this page to make as many signs as you will need for your board. Assign each member of the group at least one "stop" and one "go" reference to look up. From their reading, they should be able to write a DO idea on their GO sign and a DON'T idea on their STOP sign. Arrange all the signs on the board and read and discuss them aloud together.

STOP!!

1 Tim. 6:15
1 Tim. 5:1
1 Tim. 5:22
1 Tim. 6:17
2 Tim. 1:8
2 Tim. 2:16
2 Tim. 2:23
2 Tim. 2:24
Rom. 12:2
Rom. 12:16
Rom. 12:17
Rom. 12:21
1 Cor. 6:10
Eph. 6:14
Eph. 4:26
Eph. 5:15
James 1:27
James 1:19
James 2:8

GO!!

Eph. 5:19
Eph. 6:1
2 Cor. 9:9
Rom. 12:12
Heb. 13:2
1 Tim. 6:20
Philem. 2:14
Philem. 4:4
Col. 3:13
2 Thess. 3:12
2 Thess. 5:14
1 Peter 3:17
Matt. 5:44
Eph. 4:32
2 Tim. 2:22
Col. 2:2

IT PLEASES THE LORD WHEN WE DO THE RIGHT THING.

I ONCE HELPED AN ELDERLY COCKERPOO ACROSS THE STREET DURING THE RUSH HOUR.

RUN FROM EVIL

LOVE YOUR NEIGHBOR

BE KIND TO STRANGERS

OBEY YOUR PARENTS

YOUR ENEMIES

NOTE: A very long DO or DON'T may be written on several signs which are joined together.

187

STRANGE HAPPENINGS in SCRIPTURE

BULLETIN BOARD

MARY KAY! WHAT WAS THE MOST UNUSUAL THING THAT HAPPENED IN THE BIBLE?

Look up these stories in the Bible. Assign each member of the group one story to illustrate and retell in his own words. Arrange the stories and pictures on the board so that everyone may enjoy the strange and unusual happenings.

WHEN GOD MADE THE WHOLE WIDE WORLD IN 6 TEENY DAYS!

AND WHEN HE WAS FINISHED HE DIDN'T HAVE A WHOLE BUNCH OF JUNK TO CLEAN UP!!

Hungry lions won't eat! (Dan. 6)
A fish pays taxes! (Matt. 17:24-27)
A fire doesn't burn! (Dan. 3)
A donkey talks (Num. 22:21-38)
The sun stops (Josh. 10)
A stick turns into a snake
 (Exod. 7:6-13)
A rock gives water (Exod. 17:1-7)
Birds feed a prophet (1 Kings 17)
Trumpets make a wall fall down!
 (Josh. 6:1-20)
A jar refills automatically (2 Kings 4)
It rains food! (Exod. 16)

189

BULLETIN BOARD

Ps. 100:2
Prov. 8:33
Exod. 20:12
Gal. 5:13
Matt. 5:44
Rom. 13:1, 3

Heb. 13:7
Ps. 40:16
Matt. 22:37
Rom. 12:20
Luke 6:28
Exod. 20:18

Heb. 12:8-11
Prov. 17:17
Prov. 3:31
2 Tim. 2:5 RSV
Heb. 11:6
Mark 12:17

1 Chron. 28:9
2 Tim. 2:23
Prov. 1:8
Luke 6:27
Rom. 13:9-10
1 Tim. 4:12

1 Chron. 16:29
2 Tim. 2:15
Col. 3:13
Eph. 6:1
1 Cor. 13:4-5
Prov. 3:28-29
Eccl. 3:1, 4-5, 7
Prov. 12:1
Ps. 144:15
Prov. 18:24

Getting Along with God and Others

Keys to Successful Living with Other Human Beings and With God

.HOW COME ALL US KIDS GET ALONG SO WELL?

EVERYBODY IN THIS CRAFT BOOK GETS ALONG VERY WELL!!

Make your bulletin board look like the one on this page. Under each heading, use a row of cup hooks for hanging keys. Use the key pattern to trace and cut as many keys as you will need. Copy each reference listed here on one key. Then look it up in your Bible to find out in which column of keys it fits. Hang it in the right place on your board.

ALMOST EVERY-BODY!

NOTE: Some keys will fit in several categories. Choose the category where you think each one best fits.

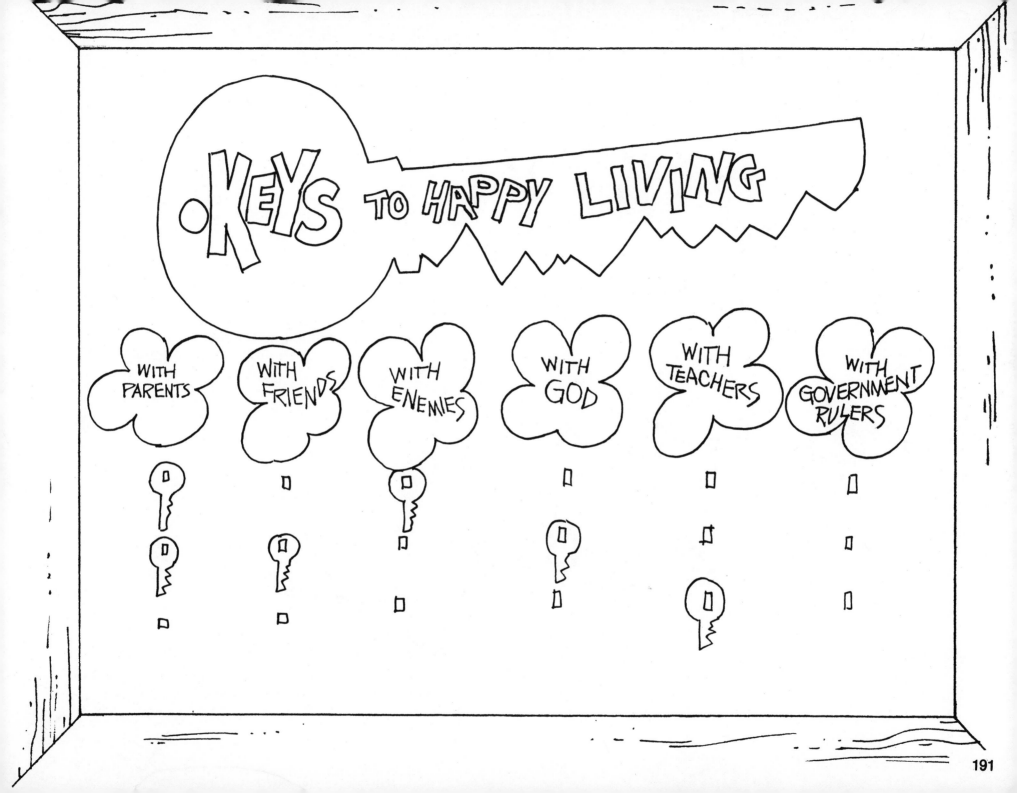

BULLETIN BOARD

Free the Prisoners

Make a bulletin board like this one that shows eight men behind bars. Two of them are chained together. Find out who they all are by "reading" their identification tags. Then "free" each one by saying his name and telling what his crime was. Did you notice that there is something similar about all eight "crimes?"

BULLETIN BOARD

Bible Riddle Board

Make a riddle board like the one on this page. (Trace the Riddler on an overhead projector, if you like. Be sure to make him a pocket in which to keep the answer envelope!) Write these riddles on rainbow-colored construction paper and mount them attractively on the board. Copy each answer on a separate slip of paper, tuck them into an envelope and put them in the Riddler's pocket. Try the riddles on your friends, classmates, and visitors!

RIDDLES

He was not afraid
Of anything
He shot a giant
With his sling!
(David)

Animals came
In 2s and 7s
And a rainbow hung
Across the heavens.
(Noah)

Tossed to the sea,
He met a fish
Who had him for
His meal's main dish!
(Jonah)

A piece of wool
Left overnight
Told him which
   choice was wrong
And which was right.
(Gideon)

He lay his head
Upon the ground,
Saw angels going
Up and down.
(Jacob)

No guns, but people
Marching around
And horns, brought
   the walls
Of this city down.
(Jericho)

The son of David,
And a great, wise
   king . . .
But he lost touch
   with God . . .
What a sad thing!
(Solomon)

When God promised
   descendants
He was old and had
   none . . .
Then later God told him
To murder his son.
(Abraham)

God made him the
   keeper
Of a lovely Creation;
His rib was the scene
Of the first operation.
(Adam)

No women's lib needed,
A prophetess, she
Was a judge who held
   court
Under a tree!
(Deborah)

Her cousin Mary was the
Girl God did choose,
But he brought her and
   her husband
Some very good news!
(Elisabeth)

God allowed Satan
To take this man's wife,
His wealth and his
   health
But NOT take his life.
(Job)

Sold by his brothers,
Loved by his dad,
Enslaved by a king,
He returned good for
   bad.
(Joseph)

She hid two spies
And gave them hope.
They later saved her
By the sign of a rope.
(Rahab)

A king he became
When he was just
   eight.
At the bow of an
   archer
He met his fate.
(Josiah)

When Jesus came
   visiting,
This gal preferred
To cook while her
   sister
Just treasured His
   Word.
(Martha)

A captive, but friend
   of the king,
He did call
All of his countrymen
To build back the
   wall!
(Nehemiah)

He sneaked to talk
To Jesus at night
And asked questions
   on how
To make his life right.
(Nicodemus)

They sold their goods
To help those in need
But they lied to God
And died for their
   deed.
(Ananias and Sapphira)

A member of Jesus'
Disciple band
Who could not believe
Till he touched His
   hand.
(Thomas)

BULLETIN BOARD

ANSWERS TO HARD QUESTIONS

Finding Answers to Hard Questions

Make a bulletin board full of questions like these and additional ones of your own. Ask each member of the group to choose two or three questions to "research." He/she may ask other Christians, read the Bible and other books, pray and discuss the questions — then bring an answer for each question back to the group. Invite other group members to add their ideas.

NOTE: A good way to do some "research" is to ask an adult Sunday school class if you can visit their class with your list of questions. Each kid questions one or two adults and records their ideas. Then the kids return to their own classroom and discuss the "adult" ideas they have recorded.

BULLETIN BOARD

Birthday Gifts for Jesus

WHAT'S IN YOUR BOX FOR JESUS?

A HAPPY HEART!

MINE!

TO JESUS

FOR JESUS

Birthday Gifts for Jesus at Christmas

Make your bulletin board look like a huge Christmas package. Ask each person in your group to think of something he could give to Jesus for his birthday, write what his gift will be on a piece of paper, and tuck it in a small box wrapped with gift wrapping paper. Attach all the gift boxes to the board until a day near Christmas when you open them together to share with your friends your gifts to Jesus.

GOD AS OUR POWER SOURCE FOR DAILY LIVING!

God As Our Power Source for Daily Living

Copy this powerful title to head your board. Then fill the board with Scripture promises that assure a special supply of power for everyday living. (Below are some suggested references to read.) Write each promise on a light bulb shape like the pattern. Color it yellow to show that you are "plugged" in to the great power source — God.

Num. 23:19	Luke 21:15	Heb. 10:16-17
Josh. 1:9	John 11:25	2 Cor. 6:17-18
Ps. 23:4	Luke 18:27	James 4:8
Gen. 9:15-16	John 16:22-23	Ps. 46:1
Isa. 1:18	Acts 2:21	Philem. 4:19
Matt. 7:8	2 Peter 3:13	James. 5:16
Matt. 11:28-30	Acts 2:38	2 Chron. 7:14
Mark 9:23	Ezek. 36:26-28	Matt. 10:32
Luke 1:37	Prov. 3:6	

A Perfect Creation

ANYTHING WE CAN DO, GOD CAN DO BETTER!!!!!!!
Think of anything human beings can do—then think about how God does it! Make a board like the one on this page that shows all the things you have thought of. Many people can contribute ideas and drawings to the board. Read the finished board together and sing or say a thank you to God!

JUST THINK OF HOW GOOD GOD IS AT MAKING THINGS!

AND JUST THINK!,,, HE MADE EVERYTHING TO FIT JUST PERFECTLY!

I DON'T THINK MY HAIRS FIT PERFECTLY!

BULLETIN BOARD

Matching Bible Couples

(A good board for the Valentine season!)

Make a huge, heart-shaped bulletin board. Make sixteen pairs of small hearts. Write one Bible lover's name on each heart. Place all of the small hearts on the board. Use tacks or pins and red or white yarn or ribbon to connect each pair of lovers.

Adam and Eve
Abraham and Sarah
Isaac and Rebekah
Jacob and Rachel
Samson and Delilah
Boaz and Ruth
Amram and Jochebed
David and Bathsheba

King Ahasuerus and Esther
Ahab and Jezebel
Joseph and Mary
Zacharias and Elisabeth
Ananias and Sapphira
Aquila and Priscilla
Hosea and Gomer
Abigail and Nabal

BULLETIN BOARD

SCRIPTURES FOR HARD TIMES

Ask your pharmacist for some prescription labels and some large, empty gelatin capsules. Use the labels to write prescriptions on small boxes or bottles like the ones on this board. Attach the boxes and bottles to your board. Then write these references and their corresponding verses on tiny strips of paper, roll each one tightly, and slide it into a gelatin capsule. (Make several capsules containing each verse.) Now, drop the capsules into the proper boxes or jars. Invite your friends, family, visitors, etc., to take a pill for whatever makes their day go wrong.

for lazy spells (1 Chron. 22:16)
for depression (Ps. 118:24 OR Job 37:14)
to fight temptation (Luke 22:40)
for weakness (Isa. 40:31)
for a troubled spirit (Phil. 4:6-7)
for a down-in-the-dumps feeling (Prov. 17:22)
for uncertainty (Rom. 8:28)
for lack of direction (Prov. 3:5-6)
for worldly pressures (John 16:33)
for weariness (Matt. 11:28 OR Gal. 6:9)
to control fear (Ps. 56:3)
for anger (Eph. 4:26)

A WORD PUZZLE

BULLETIN BOARD

LOOK OUT, WART! I'M GONNA DO A MAXI WORD-FIND PUZZLE!

Make a large word-find puzzle exactly like the one on this page. Cut out each letter from construction paper—make the letters all different colors. Print the list of clues below. Ask your friends to find at least thirty Bible words in this puzzle. Then do some more puzzles of your own.

Note: Answers to this puzzle can be found in the appendix.

CLUES:

The Heavenly Father
His Son
God's Word
One of God's very first acts
Gabriel and Michael
Follower of Jesus
Givers of wool
Our Saviour
"But the greatest of these is . . ."
Shepherd, giant-slayer, king
Christ died on one
Great gladness or delight
To talk with God
She listened to a serpent
What God hates most
Brother of Abel
The first man
Led wise men to Jesus
Loved her mother-in-law
Hid two spies
Had a donkey who talked
The city Jonah feared
Built an ark
Abraham's nephew
Lost everything but his life
Nicodemus
The world's oldest man
Its walls came down!
Joseph's youngest brother

MAXI WORD FIND PUZZLE

```
R P V B W D K F M A B E N J A M I N
E C R E A T I O N U M L J E Q E N I
S H E W T C V R C R H T U R U T E A
J R K V Y O R G O D X R P I I H O G
B I B L E Y M I W C A I N C L U J A
H S R U A L O V E T X O R H A S I N
A T G R K P J E S U S F J O B E K O
R B P K M H I W Y G P R Z G A L L R
D I S C I P L E R Z F T O L L A M B
A H Y R X A G H G S A M (N O A H) N Z
V N Y O B A N G E L S N O R A H A B
I C P S J M E X B A I P Q R M A D A
D B Z S H E E P D M B H E V E N I N
```

PATTERNS

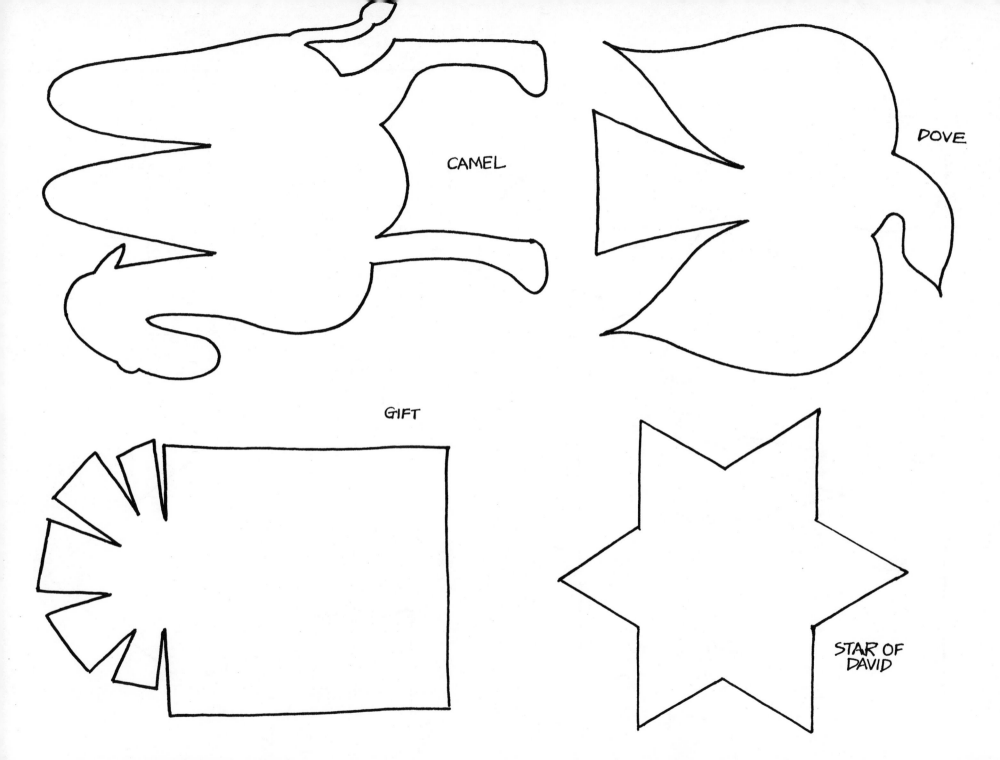

CAMEL

DOVE

GIFT

STAR OF
DAVID

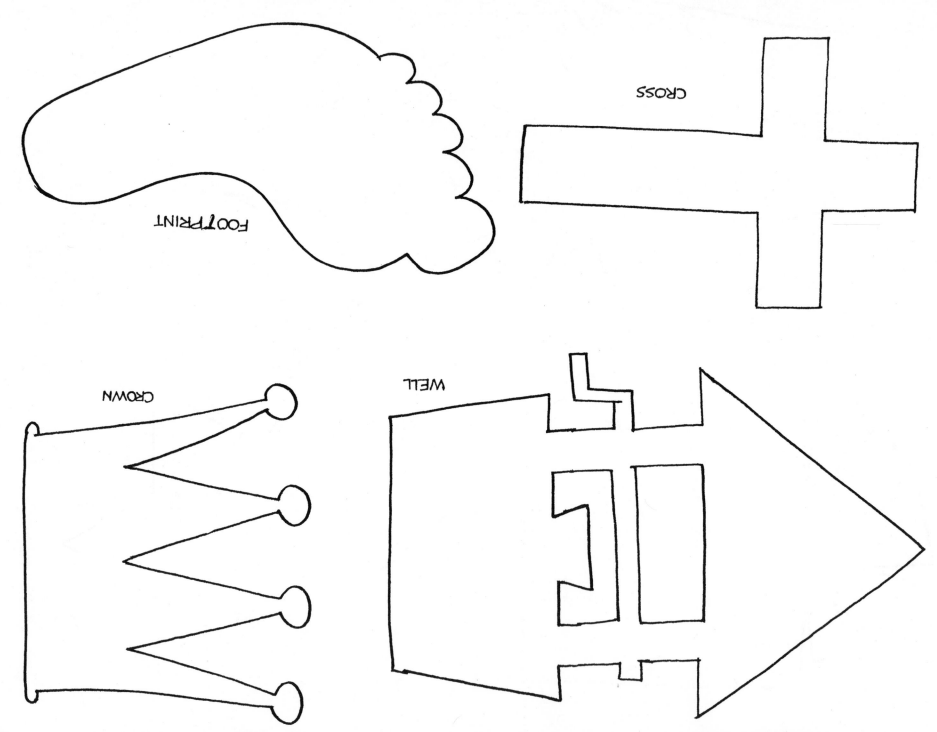

FOOTPRINT

CROSS

CROWN

WELL

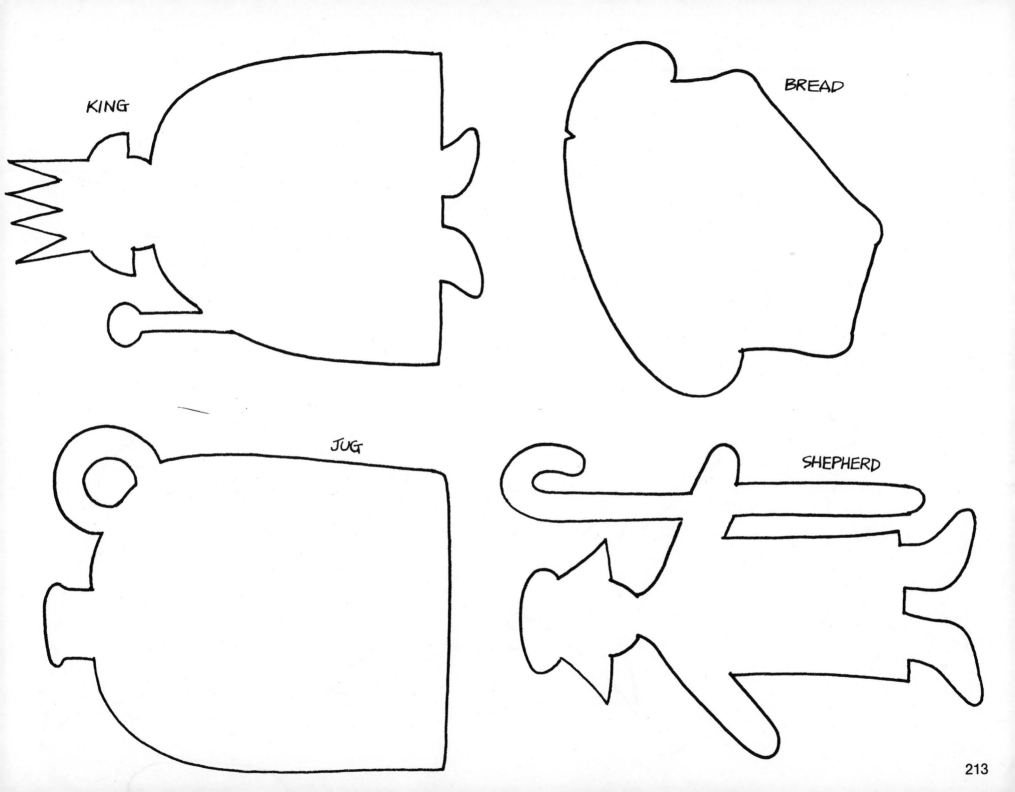

KING

BREAD

JUG

SHEPHERD

213

TREE

BEE

PINE TREE

BIRD

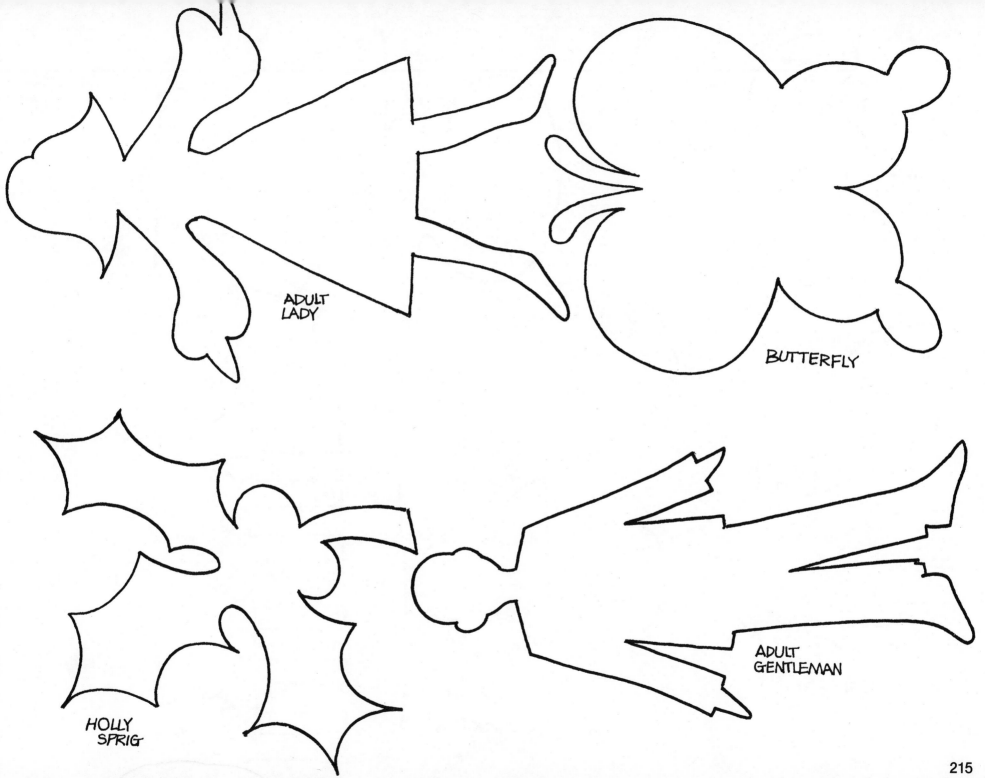

ADULT
LADY

BUTTERFLY

HOLLY
SPRIG

ADULT
GENTLEMAN

215

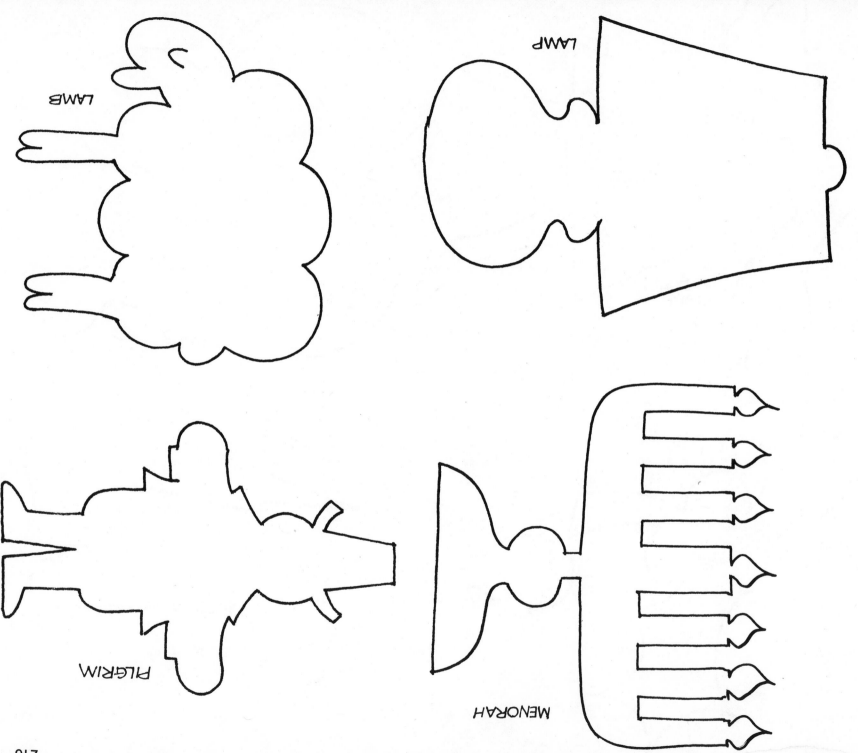

LAMB

LAMP

PILGRIM

MENORAH

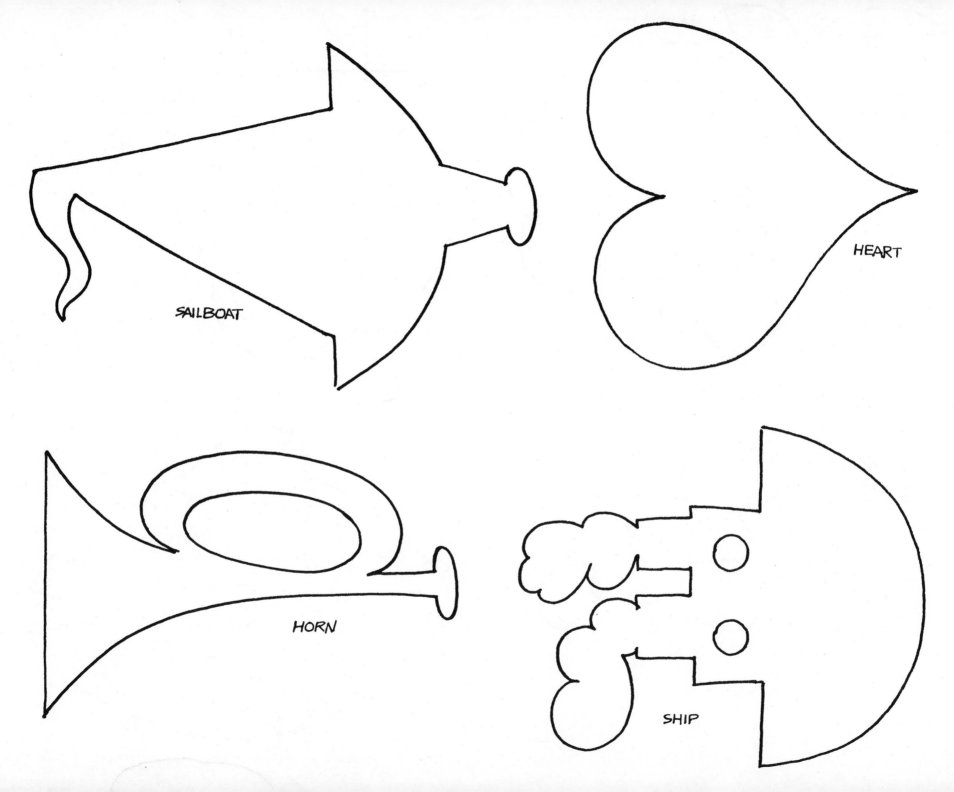

SAILBOAT

HEART

HORN

SHIP

LION

CANDLE

FLOWERS

FISH

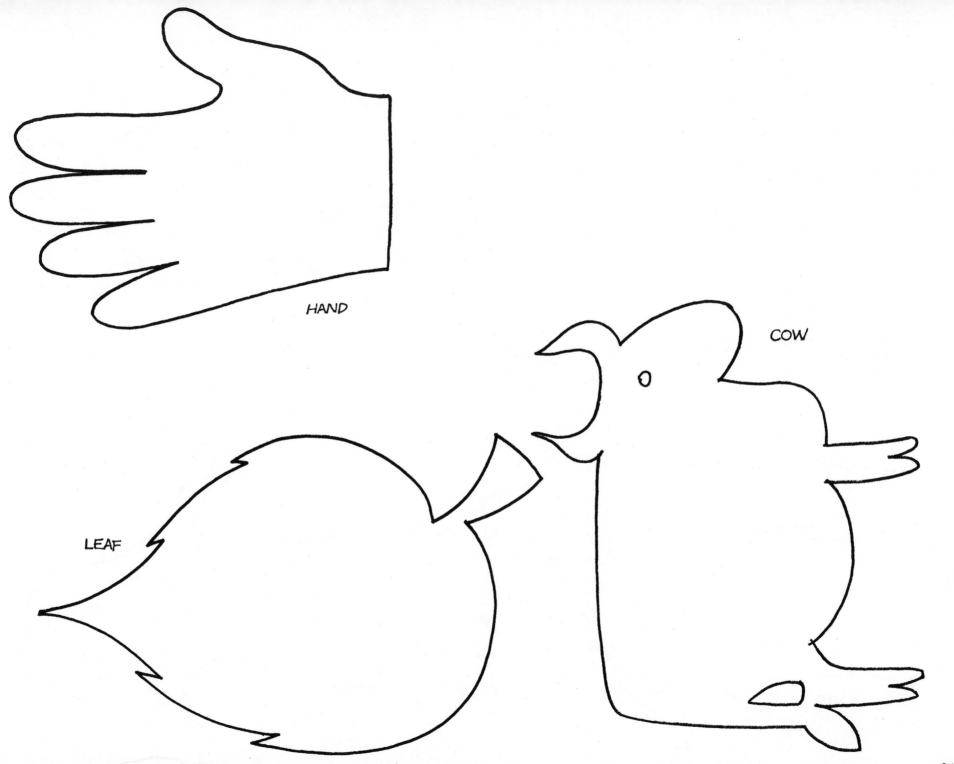

HAND

COW

LEAF

219

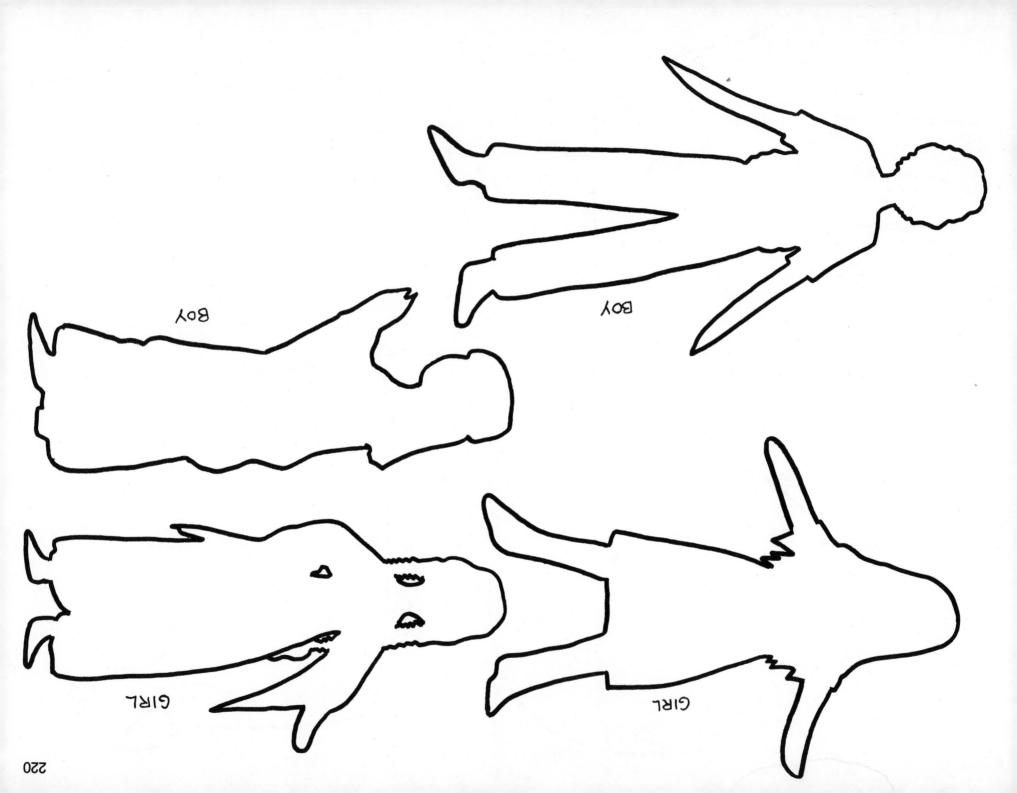

BOY

BOY

GIRL

GIRL

INDEX

ACKNOWLEDGMENT!?"!
The author is aware that thanksgiving messages of this sort are usually offered at the beginning of a book. Placing it here is not to make it appear as an after-thought; rather it is to say that last, but MOST, rather than least, do I appreciate the competent, supportive assistance of my superfriend, Shirley Bledsoe. Without her, the preparation of this manuscript could not have been nearly so efficient nor half as much fun!